D1709751

THE LIBRARY OF
AMERICAN
LIVES AND TIMES™

MERIWETHER LEWIS
AND
WILLIAM CLARK

The Corps of Discovery and the Exploration of the American Frontier

Michael D. Fox and Suzanne G. Fox

The Rosen Publishing Group's
PowerPlus Books™
New York

For Joel Schindel

Published in 2005 by The Rosen Publishing Group, Inc.
29 East 21st Street, New York, NY 10010

First Edition

Editor's Note: All quotations have been reproduced as they appeared in the letters and diaries from which they were borrowed. No correction was made to the inconsistent spelling that was common in that time period.

Library of Congress Cataloging-in-Publication Data

Fox, Michael D.
Meriwether Lewis and William Clark : the Corps of Discovery and the exploration of the American frontier / Michael D. Fox and Suzanne G. Fox.
 v. cm. — (The library of American lives and times)
Includes bibliographical references (p.) and index.
Contents: Growing up with the country — Working for Mr. Jefferson — An old idea reconsidered — Fort Wood to Fort Clark — Fort Clark to the Pacific Ocean — Back to St. Louis — Journey's end — The legacy of the Corps of Discovery.
ISBN 1-4042-2650-8 (lib. bdg.)
1. Lewis and Clark Expedition (1804–1806)—Juvenile literature. 2. Lewis, Meriwether, 1774–1809—Juvenile literature. 3. Clark, William, 1770–1838—Juvenile literature. 4. Explorers—West (U.S.)—Biography—Juvenile literature. 5. West (U.S.)—Discovery and exploration—Juvenile literature. 6. West (U.S.)—Description and travel—Juvenile literature.
[1. Lewis and Clark Expedition (1804–1806) 2. Lewis, Meriwether, 1774–1809. 3. Clark, William, 1770–1838. 4. Explorers. 5. West (U.S.)— Discovery and exploration.] I. Fox, Suzanne G. II. Title. III. Series.
F592.7.F695 2005
917.804'2—dc22
                              [B] 2003013322

Manufactured in the United States of America

CONTENTS

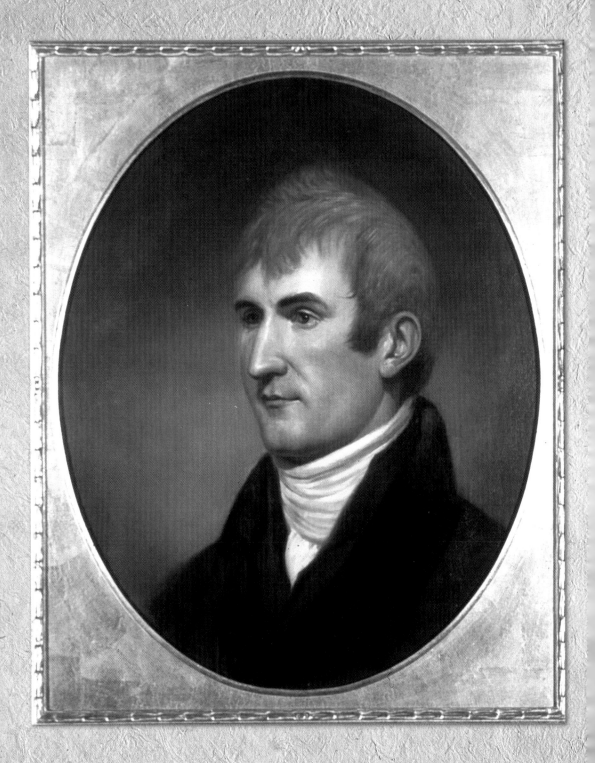

1. A Leap into the Unknown

In 1804, thirty-three people left Camp Wood, a remote spot on the upper Missouri River, on a journey westward. They would travel into lands no American had ever seen. The group, which would come to be called the Corps of Discovery, was a military organization sent by President Thomas Jefferson and paid for by the government of the United States. It eventually included woodsmen, rivermen, and a young Native American woman and her small baby, as well as soldiers. Together this group would search for a route across the continent. Members of the Corps would rely on the courtesy and assistance of the native people they encountered. They all hoped that with a little luck, they would cross the westernmost part of the United States, enter territory then held by the British, reach the Pacific Ocean, and then come back to the eastern United States.

Opposite: Charles Willson Peale made this portrait of Meriwether Lewis around 1807. Lewis was described as tall and broad-shouldered. Even before his adventurous journey, he was characterized as having "great steadiness of purpose, self-possession, and undaunted courage."

The expedition into the Louisiana Territory led by Captains Meriwether Lewis and William Clark was the first great adventure of the nineteenth century, undertaken by a very young nation. The United States had existed only since the colonists won their freedom from Great Britain in 1783. For several years after the American Revolution, the thirteen new states were loosely bound together under the Articles of Confederation. This situation ended in 1787 with the ratification of the Constitution of the United States. The Constitution outlined the responsibilities of both the state and the federal governments.

When Lewis and Clark journeyed westward, the United States had just bought the Louisiana Territory from France. This territory extended the United States' borders across most of the continent of North America. At the time, no one was quite sure where the boundaries of the Louisiana Purchase lay. When the explorers crossed into land that is now Oregon and Washington, they would be leaving behind the United States and the Louisiana Territory and entering territory held by foreign nations. Both Britain and Russia were claiming this portion of the northwest coast. Spain controlled all of what is now California and the southwest, as well as Mexico.

Opposite: Charles Willson Peale made this portrait of William Clark around 1810. Lewis and Clark were described as having personalities with complementary strengths and weaknesses. Their differences helped them to deal with many situations that they encountered.

Throughout their lives, both Lewis and Clark had strong familial and political ties to Virginia. Lewis and Clark, like most others in Virginia, believed that Virginians were superior to other Americans. Virginia was the first colony that the British established on American soil. Virginians had the biggest plantations, the finest houses, the best horses, the most African slaves, and the most wealth and political power of any Americans. There were fine colleges, grand public buildings, and beautiful cities in Virginia. In addition, many Virginians had played important roles in the creation of the United States. Virginians George Washington, Thomas Jefferson, James Madison, and James Monroe had helped to lead the rebellion against the English king George III and had worked to establish the new democratic government. Of the first five presidents, four were Virginians.

Both Lewis and Clark were strongly affected by the American Revolution. Although neither had been old enough to fight in the war, both had immediate family members who had served in the Continental army. Lewis's father died of an illness he caught during his service. Five of Clark's older brothers served in the Continental army, and one of them, John, died in British captivity. George Rogers Clark, who was eighteen years older than William, became a national hero for helping the young nation to win a Revolutionary War battle in the Ohio Valley. William was very impressed with George's accomplishments. He always spoke proudly of them, even many years after the war was over. As a result of the conflict, both Lewis and Clark were always suspicious of Britain and its subjects.

As did many people at the turn of the nineteenth century, Lewis and Clark embraced the ideas of an important European philosophical movement called the Enlightenment. This philosophy said that the universe operated by unchanging laws that had been set in motion by

James Barton Longacre painted this undated portrait of George Rogers Clark. Clark was trained by his grandfather to survey land, a skill his younger brother William also learned.

God. Everything was connected by what was called the Great Chain of Being. The dust of the earth, the water of the oceans, and the plants and the animals, including humans, were bound in a dynamic order with God at the top of the chain. Believers in the Enlightenment argued that reason was the most valuable tool for understanding the laws of the universe. The scientific method of study that resulted from the Enlightenment was considered very important because it offered people systematic ways to think about the world. Scientists in Europe and the United

States were making new discoveries, and they were also developing new ways of classifying information to reflect orderliness in the universe.

Notions from the Enlightenment strongly influenced Lewis and Clark. Both were very interested in studying plants, animals, and human beings, and in describing and classifying what they learned. Both firmly believed that reason was the most useful tool that people had to help them understand the world in which they lived.

When Lewis and Clark prepared to lead their men west, they believed that they were heading into a land that resembled the biblical Garden of Eden. They expected that this land would harbor an abundance of animals that fur traders could trap, and that farmers could settle there and become prosperous. They believed that the great rivers in the Louisiana Territory connected to each other high in the mountains, which would allow people and goods to be moved from coast to coast by water. They thought that the mountains they would find would be low and easily crossed, and that on the other side the land would be flat and the climate temperate. Lewis and Clark had no idea whether their beliefs about the land would prove true, as they would be among the first white people to map this territory.

Most important, Lewis and Clark, the men who went with them, and their sponsor, the U.S. government, all had very definite ideas about the Native Americans they would meet. They believed that the way the Indians lived was inferior to the way the colonists lived. They believed that all Indian women were little better than slaves. They believed that they could easily convince Indian tribes that had been enemies for hundreds of years to become friends. The explorers were charged with informing the Indians that they had a new "Great Father," Thomas Jefferson, and that he expected them to be loyal to the United States and to live peaceably with other tribes. The captains' notions about the Indians made it nearly impossible to deliver this message.

Almost all the assumptions that Lewis and Clark had made about their journey were wrong. Looking back on the efforts of the Corps of Discovery, we can see that they accomplished many important tasks, although almost none of those were what they had been sent out to achieve. Nevertheless, what they learned about the people and the places they saw on their journey from St. Louis, Missouri, to the Pacific Ocean and back changed the course of American history.

2. Growing Up with the Country

William Clark and Meriwether Lewis were both born just a few years before the beginning of the American Revolution. According to family records, William Clark's family emigrated, or moved, from England to the colony of Virginia during the seventeenth century. Growing tobacco was the family business. John Clark III, William's father, married his second cousin, Ann Rogers, in 1749. He moved with his wife from his family's plantation in King and Queen County, Virginia, to another in Albemarle County, Virginia. It was here that the first four of their eleven children were born. The Clark home was about 1 mile (1.6 km) from that of Thomas Jefferson's, and the families remained friendly even after the Clarks moved from Albemarle County to Caroline County, Virginia, in about 1757. John and Ann's tenth child, William, was born on August 1, 1770.

When William was thirteen, his family moved to what is now Kentucky. Only a few years before, the area had been a wilderness with few European-American inhabitants. William's older brothers had been privately

Tobacco was a common crop in eighteenth-century Virginia. Slaves did the grueling field work. In this lithograph by G. Bramati from around 1790, slaves are shown preparing the tobacco for the curing process.

tutored in Virginia, but when the family moved to Kentucky, William did not have the same opportunities. There were no public schools in Kentucky, and few people had sufficient education to teach children well. All his life, William was self-conscious about his lack of formal education, but he did a good job of teaching himself by reading and studying. Since his family was living in the country, he also became an exceptional woodsman. He could ride a horse, shoot a gun, track animals and people, and find his way around the woods.

R. T. Zogbaum painted *Charge of the Dragoons at Fallen Timbers* around 1895. In the Battle of the Fallen Timbers, Wayne's decisive victory against the Northwest Indian Confederation brought about the Treaty of Fort Greenville in 1795. This gave the United States most of Ohio and parts of Indiana, Illinois, and Michigan. After the treaty, people in the United States began to settle and explore this new territory.

Inspired in part by his older brothers' military service, Clark joined the U.S. Army at the age of twenty. In 1794, he took part in the Battle of the Fallen Timbers, during which the American general "Mad" Anthony Wayne defeated the Native American tribes that lived in the territory along the Ohio River. In 1795, Clark was stationed in Ohio, where he commanded the Chosen Rifle Company, a group of sharpshooters. That year, General Wayne transferred a young ensign named Meriwether Lewis to Clark's unit.

Meriwether Lewis was born on August 18, 1774, in Albemarle County, Virginia, near present-day Charlottesville. His parents, William Lewis and Lucy Meriwether, had married in 1769. Lucy Meriwether was well read, and she knew how to use wild plants to help sick people get well. She taught young Meriwether Lewis a great deal about plants. Meriwether was the couple's second child and their first son. The couple also had a daughter, Jane, and a younger son, Reuben. Because he lived near the Lewis family, Thomas Jefferson knew both sides of the family well. He considered William Lewis a good friend.

Both the Lewis and Meriwether families had acquired a lot of property in Virginia by the time Meriwether was born. In April 1775, when the American Revolution began, William Lewis joined in the fight to free his country from English rule. William

This rifle is a reproduction of a 1792 rifle. The insignia of the U.S. Armory is inscribed on it. Both Lewis and Clark were skilled marksmen, as were many men of their time period, and they would have used a rifle such as this one.

John Neagle painted this portrait of William Lewis based on Gilbert Stuart's portrait. William Lewis served without pay in the American Revolution, seeing it as his patriotic duty to leave "all to aid in the liberation of his country."

Lewis enlisted as a member of the Albemarle County militia and was promoted to first lieutenant by September. When the unit was integrated into the Continental army, he was made a lieutenant. He was away from home serving in the war for most of the first five years of Meriwether's life.

In November 1779, William Lewis visited his family at Cloverfields, the plantation in Virginia where his wife Lucy had grown up. As he was returning to his unit, he was washed off his horse when he tried to cross the Rivanna River. Although he managed to get ashore and walk back to Cloverfields, he caught pneumonia and died two days later.

In colonial America, women had very few rights. If a woman's husband died, his property passed to the couple's children rather than to his wife. This may be one reason why a widow often remarried very soon after the death of a husband. Lucy Lewis married Captain John Marks less than six months after her husband died. She and Marks had a son, John Hastings, and a daughter, Mary Garland.

After William Lewis died, his brother, Nicholas Lewis, was appointed Meriwether's guardian. This meant that he was responsible for looking after the boy's inheritance until Meriwether could manage it himself. Meriwether had inherited Locust Hill, the family plantation, in addition to money and slaves. Nicholas Lewis took over the management of the estate for Meriwether. By all accounts, he was an honest and a careful guardian.

When Meriwether was about nine, John Marks moved the family to northeast Georgia, where several other Virginian families were settling on land near the Broad River. It was in Georgia that Meriwether began to develop the skills of an outdoorsman that served him so well in later life. He was already a good rider, and he learned to shoot, hunt, and fish along the Broad River. He spent many hours in the woods, studying the land, animals, and plants.

In those days, there were not many good public schools in the colonies, and there were none at all in Virginia. Children of wealthy families usually studied with private tutors. There were far fewer qualified teachers in Georgia than in Virginia. Meriwether wanted more formal schooling, so he returned to Virginia at age thirteen to study. The inheritance from his father's estate made Meriwether a wealthy young man, so he could afford an education.

Though there were more private tutors working in Virginia than in Georgia, the demand for their services was still so great that Meriwether had some trouble getting one. He contacted several tutors before Parson Matthew Maury took him in. Maury was the son of one of Thomas Jefferson's teachers. After studying with Maury, Meriwether went to study with Dr. Charles Everitt for one year. In 1790, the boy moved on to study with the Reverend James Waddell, remaining with him until 1792. By the time Meriwether finished his formal schooling, he had learned some Latin, ancient and British history, literature, mathematics, geography, and philosophy, and he had developed a fine, readable penmanship.

From his family and those in his social circle, Meriwether learned the other skills necessary to a successful planter and member of Virginia's finest society. He was an excellent and confident horseman and a good judge of horses. He could dance, play cards, fence, hunt, and fish. At the age of eighteen, Meriwether left his tutors to take over the management of Locust Hill from his uncle and guardian, Nicholas. The younger man's formal education was finished.

From 1792 to 1794, Meriwether Lewis ran his plantation, on which he mainly grew tobacco. His occupation involved making decisions about planting, harvesting and selling his crops, and seeing to it that the buildings and tools on the plantation were kept in good condition. African slaves did all the manual labor on the plantation. Sometime before 1794, John Marks died, and Lewis purchased some of his property. After her second husband's death, Lucy Marks returned to Locust Hill to live with her son.

Lewis was getting restless, however. He wanted to travel and explore, and the settled life of a planter could not satisfy those desires. In 1794, he got an opportunity. That year, the U.S. government established a tax on whiskey as a way to raise money to support the new nation. The taxation upset many citizens in western Pennsylvania, who believed it was an unfair burden on settlers of the western frontier.

Many of those who objected to the tax rebelled against the new government, shooting at the officers who tried to collect the tax and burning down their houses. President George Washington recognized the seriousness of this rebellion and personally led thousands of militiamen into western Pennsylvania to put it down.

Lewis enlisted as a private in the corps of Virginian volunteers when the Whiskey Rebellion broke out in 1794. As the soldiers marched toward Pittsburgh, Pennsylvania, the leaders of the rebellion fled down the Ohio River. The rebellion was successfully suppressed. Lewis stayed in Pennsylvania as part of the occupying force responsible for guarding western Pennsylvania. On May 1, 1795, Lewis joined the U.S. Army with the rank of ensign.

This decision upset his mother, who had been urging him to come home to Locust Hill and take up his responsibilities there. Lewis had gotten a taste of adventure, however, and he did not want to go back to Virginia. He was sent to Ohio to serve under General Anthony Wayne, where he took part in several important events. Probably most significant, he was present when the Indian tribes that had been defeated at the Battle of the Fallen Timbers signed the Treaty of Greenville and surrendered their ancestral lands to their conquerors. His experience in seeing how army officers negotiated with the Native Americans of the Ohio River valley would influence the ways in which he dealt with the Indians

he would meet on his future expedition.

One day, after drinking a large amount of alcohol, Ensign Lewis disrupted a gathering of officers. He was brought up on the court-martial charges of insulting an officer and challenging him to a duel. He was acquitted of the charges, but General Wayne transferred Lewis into William Clark's company to separate the quarreling officers. About six months later, Clark resigned his commission and returned home to take care of his family. For the next several years, Clark lived quietly at the family home near what is now Louisville, Kentucky,

Above: The Whiskey Rebellion was the event that required the U.S. government to exercise its authority within state boundaries. Officials were sent into western Pennsylvania to quell rioting that broke out when federal officers attempted to collect the new tax on whiskey. This anonymous 1794 engraving shows people rebelling against the tax.

taking care of business matters and helping his brother, George Rogers Clark. Lewis and Clark had spent only a short time together, but in those few months they became friends for life.

Lewis and Clark were alike in many ways. Both were Virginians, both were fine woodsmen, and both were able leaders of men. They firmly believed in military discipline and the use of reason. In spite of their similar backgrounds, however, they had very different temperaments. Clark was a modest man. Long after the Lewis and Clark expedition had been successfully completed, he was reluctant to talk about his accomplishments on the trip, but he always spoke glowingly of the exploits of his brother, George Rogers Clark, during the American Revolution. Clark was calm and slow to anger. Both his superior officers and the men who reported to him in the army respected him. He was loving and loyal to his family, and he genuinely admired what his friends and relatives achieved. Clark believed, for instance, that Lewis was a better writer than he was, and he often asked Lewis to help him when he had to write letters and reports.

Lewis was more hot-tempered than his friend, and sometimes when he got angry his reactions were more violent than those the situation called for. Many of Lewis's friends described him as "melancholy." At these times, he seemed sad and distant, and he had little to say. Lewis probably suffered from depression, which is a serious mental illness. People with depression sometimes feel so unhappy that they are unable to do everyday tasks, such as managing their affairs and looking after their families. Today the illness can be treated with medicines and therapy. In Meriwether Lewis's time, doctors had little understanding of the variety of conditions they grouped under the general name of "melancholy." There was no way to determine if a person had this problem, let alone any way to treat it.

To make matters worse, Lewis drank a lot of alcohol, which is a depressive drug. In a time when many men customarily drank great quantities of alcohol, Lewis was noted to have been a particularly heavy drinker. Regardless of whether he suffered from depression, the amount he drank was not good for his health.

Lewis remained in the army until 1801. During that time he delivered dispatches for General Wayne to officers at various army posts. This led him to travel widely throughout what was then the western United States. The notion of what was considered the West in the United States has always depended on where the western boundary of the country was at the time. At the turn of the nineteenth century, the United States extended as far west as the Mississippi River. These traveling experiences greatly improved Lewis's frontier

_____

Next page: This map from the 1790s shows North America from the Mississippi River to the Pacific Ocean. The Northwest Territory was created by Congress in 1787 to include the area west of Pennsylvania and east of the Mississippi River. One of the goals of the Lewis and Clark expedition was to create more precise maps of the growing country.

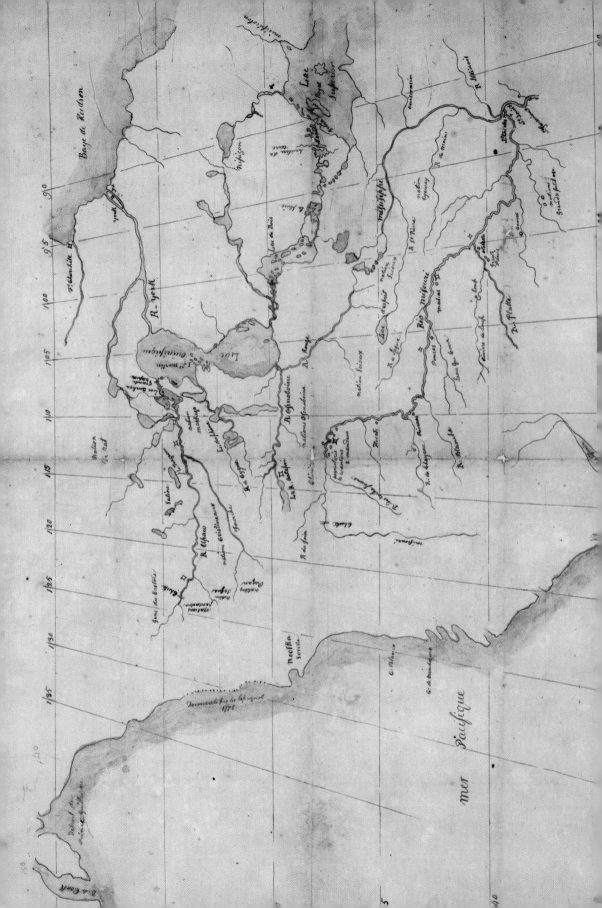

skills. On March 3, 1799, Lewis was promoted to lieutenant and sent to serve as a recruiter in Charlottesville, close to his family home. Soon after his promotion, he became a regimental paymaster, which required him to travel around the Northwest Territory distributing wages to various units in his regiment. While he had this job, he learned a great deal about the territory west of the Appalachian Mountains, and he also met almost all the officers who were stationed in the west.

On December 5, 1800, Lewis was promoted to captain. In February of the next year, Thomas Jefferson was elected president of the United States. His election would change the lives of Meriwether Lewis and William Clark forever.

3. Working for President Jefferson

On February 23, 1801, Thomas Jefferson wrote to Captain Meriwether Lewis, who was stationed in Pittsburgh, Pennsylvania. Jefferson had known Lewis since his boyhood because the Lewis family lived nearby. Virginia was a close-knit southern community and over the years the president-elect had kept up with what was going on in Lewis's career.

Jefferson, who would be sworn into office on March 4, invited Lewis to come to Washington and become his secretary. The job would make Lewis responsible for communicating the president's views and wishes to Congress. Beyond this primary duty, Lewis was to assist the president in researching questions related to the operation of the government. He would meet with members of Congress, soldiers, and citizens, each of whom had an opinion on the issues that the president

Opposite: Rembrandt Peale painted this oil-on-canvas portrait of Thomas Jefferson in 1805. Jefferson was the third president of the United States. The purchase of the Louisiana Territory is regarded as one of the boldest presidential actions in American history.

had to deal with every day. As payment for his services, Lewis would receive $500 per year, would be given the use of a servant and a horse, and would live in the President's House, which became known as the White House in 1812. Jefferson also assured Lewis that he could retain his rank and his right to promotion in the army.

Lewis accepted the position immediately and with great pleasure. He left Pittsburgh at once, but it took him three weeks to reach Washington. He traveled on horseback, and both the roads and the weather were bad. Once he arrived, Lewis moved into the President's House, where he would live for the next two years. The mansion had twenty-three big, cold, drafty rooms. For most of the time that Lewis worked for Jefferson, he and the president lived there with eleven servants to look after them and the house. Jefferson's wife had died several years before, and his two grown daughters had families of their own.

Lewis spent most of his time attending to Jefferson's visitors and calling on members of Congress with messages and information from the president. Jefferson also planned to reduce the size of the army by half, so Lewis worked very hard reviewing the records of all the officers and making recommendations about who should stay in the service and who should be dismissed. Lewis already knew practically all the army's officers in the West, but this task familiarized him with many

Samuel Blodget drew this picture of the President's House around 1800. Architect James Hoban designed the President's House, which is the oldest federal building in Washington, D.C.

John Adams, the second president, was the first chief executive to live in what was known as the President's House at 1600 Pennsylvania Avenue in Washington, D.C. When he and his wife, Abigail, moved into the large house in the fall of 1800, it was still under construction. It is said that Mrs. Adams hung her laundry up to dry in the East Room, where Meriwether Lewis slept a few years later. During the War of 1812, the British set fire to the President's House. After it was repaired, it became known as the White House because of the way the new sandstone contrasted with the surrounding brick buildings. President Theodore Roosevelt officially gave that name to the residence in 1902. Over the past 200 years, the White House has been extensively renovated several times, but the exterior stone walls are still the original construction. Today the residence has 132 rooms and 35 bathrooms on 6 levels.

others who were stationed in different parts of the country. He also learned a lot about the inner workings of the army as a whole.

Lewis ate his meals with Jefferson and was often present when the president had guests for dinner. The president regularly hosted small parties of as many as a dozen guests, and notable people from many professions were invited to dine with him. On any evening, Lewis might have sat down with members of Jefferson's cabinet; members of Congress; celebrated artists; philosophers; important members of society from Washington, D.C., or other places; foreign ambassadors; and clergymen.

Jefferson and Lewis spent a lot of time alone together, too, so Lewis had plenty of opportunities to talk to the president. Jefferson was one of the most remarkable intellectuals of his, or any, age. He studied history, languages, astronomy, botany, architecture, zoology, mineralogy, and anthropology. He was also the most famous promoter of the Enlightenment and of scientific thinking in American society. Jefferson was not interested in making public speeches, but he was a gifted storyteller, and people loved to hear him talk.

At a time when books were rare and expensive, Jefferson owned one of the most important and varied private libraries in North America. As his personal secretary Lewis was free to read anything in it. Living and working with Thomas Jefferson must have been fascinating for the younger man, who had only a basic education. Lewis was able to learn from someone who knew much about many different subjects.

The time that Lewis spent as Jefferson's secretary undoubtedly changed his life. Aside from learning a great deal about philosophy and science, Lewis got the chance to see firsthand the way that government and politics worked.

Jefferson would serve two terms as president. During his presidency, events were taking shape in Europe that would persuade Jefferson that his young nation was ready for a great expansion in territory. An opportunity was about to present itself to Jefferson, and his actions would ultimately guide the course of America's future in a very dramatic way. Jefferson's, and America's, great opportunity would result in Lewis's leaving the president for a great adventure in the West.

4. An Old Idea Reconsidered

Thomas Jefferson came to believe that it was the destiny of the United States to extend from the Atlantic Ocean to the Pacific Ocean. When he became president in 1801, the country's westernmost border was the Mississippi River. To the west was Louisiana, which the French had controlled for years until the French king, Louis XV, had turned it over to his cousin, Carlos IV king of Spain, in 1762. For nearly forty years, the Spanish controlled the Mississippi River, from the crucial port of New Orleans on the Gulf of Mexico to the growing trading settlement of St. Louis, just south of where the Missouri River enters the Mississippi River.

Spain was not very active in Louisiana, but on the European continent, Napoléon Bonaparte, the leader of France, was building an empire. When Spain suddenly handed Louisiana back to France in 1801, Jefferson was immediately worried that Napoléon might be planning to send his armies into his newly acquired American lands. At that time, the Mississippi River was the main highway for commerce into the interior of the

François Gérard painted this portrait of Napoléon Bonaparte (1769–1821) around 1804, just after Jefferson purchased the Louisiana Territory from France. Napoléon was a French general who became the country's leader following the French Revolution and who later crowned himself emperor of France.

American continent. Practically everything that set-tlers in the extreme western United States needed in the way of manufactured goods had to come either down the Ohio River from the east, or down the Atlantic coast and then up the Mississippi River through the port at New Orleans. The president decided to try to buy New Orleans from Napoléon Bonaparte to protect American access to the Mississippi River.

Jefferson had long wanted to send explorers into Louisiana, and, as he was negotiating for a portion of it, he thought about an expedition more seriously. Jefferson was eager for American explorers to discover the Northwest Passage. For centuries people had thought that the coastal rivers of North America connected somewhere in the interior of the continent, so that it would be possible to travel across the entire landmass by water. If such a passage existed, the nation that controlled it would be able to open a valuable trade route to Asia.

In 1793, Alexander Mackenzie, a Scottish explorer, had crossed Canada from east to west and reached the Pacific Ocean. Mackenzie had not discovered the Northwest Passage, but Jefferson thought it was only a matter of time before somebody did. He wanted American explorers to find it first, so that the United States could control traffic on the entire waterway, not just on the Mississippi River. Jefferson began planning an expedition that would make the journey westward, across Louisiana and beyond. Because he was interested in the natural sciences, Jefferson also wanted to learn about the terrain, plants, animals, and peoples of Louisiana. Though he would not accompany the expedition himself, the president knew that sending someone who knew something about natural science would be important to acquiring the knowledge he sought.

Jefferson chose his secretary, Meriwether Lewis, to lead the expedition. Lewis's expertise as a woodsman and his knowledge of the Northwest Territory led the president to believe that Lewis would make a fine commander. Because no one had ever made such a journey before, the preparations for the expedition were complicated. Lewis was responsible for gathering all the equipment and supplies that his men would need. He had to buy weapons, and presents for the Indians that they would meet along the way. Lewis began drawing up lists of needed items. His first budget was for $2,500.

During their conversations about the expedition, Lewis and Jefferson also decided that once the group reached the upper Missouri River, the waters would be too shallow for the boats that had taken them that far. They realized that the Corps would need to have different types of boats to accommodate the conditions and situations they would encounter on their journey. The president and his secretary designed a collapsible boat with an iron frame that could travel well in shallow water. The frame could be packed up in sections and

The Corps designed and built several types of boats during their
journey. Keith Rocco's 2002 drawing shows members of the Corps
(*from left to right*: Joseph Field, Meriwether Lewis, Patrick Gass, and John
Shields) stretching leather skins over an iron-frame boat. Gass wrote
that, when put in the water, the boat floated "like a perfect cork."
This boat, called the "Experiment," later began to leak.

carried up the Missouri River, where the pieces would
be fitted together and covered with animal hides.

Lewis had no formal training as a scientist, so
Jefferson began to teach him botany, geography, mineralogy, astronomy, and ethnology. In the spring of
1803, Jefferson was ready to send Lewis away to begin
gathering supplies. Lewis left Washington, D.C., on
March 15, stopping first at the U.S. Army Armory at
Harpers Ferry, Virginia. There he bought fifteen U.S.

Model 1803 rifles, some pipe tomahawks, and knives for the trip. He also got a crew started on building the collapsible iron boat. Then Lewis went on to Lancaster, Pennsylvania, where he worked with Andrew Ellicott, an important astronomer and mathematician. Ellicott taught the future explorer celestial navigation, a method of determining one's location by taking readings of the positions of the Sun and the stars using precise instruments. Lewis then went to Philadelphia, where he studied with a scientist named Robert Patterson and with Dr. Benjamin Rush, who advised him on medical matters. He also worked with Dr. Benjamin Smith Barton, a physician and botanist, and

Clark used this compass *(left)* during the expedition. He used it to keep an accurate record of the Corps' progress and to measure the distances for the map he would make for President Jefferson. The compass's case is on the right.

Chronometers were known for being delicate and complicated to use. This may explain why the Corps had trouble with the chronometer they brought on the expedition.

Most of the maps of the western United States that existed when Jefferson and Lewis began planning the expedition showed few details. Jefferson wanted Lewis and Clark to make accurate maps of the country, so the captains brought along scientific instruments to help them to do this. Among these instruments were compasses and a pocket chronometer.

The pocket chronometer was a type of a watch that was used to determine longitude. The chronometer was the most expensive item Lewis purchased for the trip. He paid $250 for it. Despite the care he took with it, it never worked properly. Sometimes it stopped altogether. The weather to which it was exposed, which ranged from wet to dry and dusty, plus the vibrations it endured as the Corps traveled, might have damaged the delicate parts of the timepiece.

with Dr. Caspar Wistar, who taught anatomy at the University of Pennsylvania and was an expert on fossils.

In Lancaster, Pennsylvania, Lewis also shopped for the expedition. He bought rifles, lead shot and gunpowder, a chronometer, beads, scissors, knives, trinkets for the Indians, paper and ink, and food. He also bought books, medicines, mosquito netting, oilskin bags, candles, fishhooks, and oiled linen for tents.

In June, Lewis returned to Washington, D.C. Jefferson had written detailed and lengthy instructions for the expedition and circulated them among his cabinet members for their comments. He and Lewis then worked on the final version of the instructions together. At some point in their conversations, they agreed that the expedition would need another officer. On June 19, Lewis wrote to his friend William Clark, inviting him to join in the journey. Clark accepted the invitation immediately.

On July 4, 1803, the day before Meriwether Lewis planned to leave Washington, D.C., he learned that Thomas Jefferson had purchased the entire Louisiana Territory in early May for $15 million. This development made Lewis and Clark's expedition even more important. Now they would be exploring the land with the idea of learning what value it might have to the United States. Almost immediately, Jefferson was criticized for spending so much money for land that many thought was probably unfit for either settlement or farming. The expedition would have to do its best to prove otherwise.

This political cartoon from around 1806 is an etching with watercolor by James Akin. It criticizes Thomas Jefferson's plans to add to his Louisiana Purchase by secretly negotiating in 1804 to buy parts of Florida from Spain. Jefferson is shown as a dog vomiting gold coins at the feet of a diplomat.

Lewis started out the next day for Pittsburgh, Pennsylvania. He quickly ran into trouble. When he reached Fredericktown, today's Frederick, Maryland, he discovered that the driver of the wagon carrying supplies for the expedition had not brought the firearms from Harpers Ferry with him. Lewis had to find someone else to go back and pick up the guns as well as the frame of the iron boat that he and Jefferson had designed.

Lewis went back to Harpers Ferry, where he looked over the firearms. Then he left for Pittsburgh. There a local builder was supposed to finish work on the wide wooden boat that would carry Lewis and the expedition's supplies down the Ohio River. The boat was to have been ready by July 20. Even though Lewis nagged the builder continuously, it was the end of August before the boat was finished and Lewis could leave.

By then, the Ohio River was low, and Lewis was afraid that the boat would run aground. To lighten his boat, he sent a lot of his supplies and equipment by wagon to Wheeling, which was then in Virginia, and he set out in his wooden boat with a crew of rivermen whom he had hired to take him down the river. That night he also began one of the tasks that Jefferson had assigned him for the trip—Lewis made the first entry in the journal that he kept for the entire journey.

Despite the hard rains that fell on Lewis and his men while they were going down the Ohio River, the water level remained so low that they were often in danger of running aground. Several times they had to unload most of their goods and hire local farmers to cart the supplies over land past the low spots in the river. They spent many hours unpacking their goods, laying them out to dry so that they could be carried over land, and then repacking them.

On the Ohio River, mosquitoes made their first appearance, and the pesky insects were a part of the expedition from then on. Besides being bothersome, they carried malaria, a serious disease that causes high fevers, sweating, and delirium. Lewis carried medicines with him that contained quinine, which treated the symptoms of malaria, but which did not cure the disease.

It took about one month for Lewis to reach Cincinnati, Ohio. There the Ohio River runs along what is now the boundary between Ohio and Kentucky. Lewis met Clark in Clarksville, Indiana, just across the Ohio River from Louisville, Kentucky, which is a little west of Cincinnati. There the two captains met to assemble the men of the expedition. The group included about twenty-five soldiers and recruits, George Drouillard, who served as an interpreter and a scout, Clark's servant and slave, York, and Lewis's Newfoundland dog, Seaman. Lewis and Clark wanted brave, sturdy young men with the skills to survive in the wilderness and a taste for adventure. The group that they assembled proved for the most part to be equal to the task.

The expedition moved up the Mississippi River to a site about 27 miles (43.5 km) northeast of St. Louis, near present-day Wood River, Illinois. There they camped for the winter. They ordered the men to build huts for shelter. They established a military routine, training their men to march, making them practice shooting, and getting themselves ready for the trip ahead. They also wrote in their journals regularly. Besides the two captains, four of the men, Charles Floyd, John Ordway, Robert Frazier, and Patrick Gass, also kept journals.

Lewis also spent quite a bit of time in St. Louis visiting prominent citizens, hiring a few additional men for the trip, and buying even more supplies. Lewis and Clark rarely both left their camp at the same time, however. Someone had to stay to maintain proper military discipline. As the winter progressed, all the men, including the two captains, were beginning to get restless. They could not begin their journey until the winter weather broke, they had the supplies they needed, and the river was free of ice.

Although Clark sometimes wrote observations on scrap paper, he also wrote in his elkskin-bound journal.

5. Fort Wood to Fort Mandan

On March 9, 1804, Meriwether Lewis and William Clark attended the event at which the formal transfer of the Louisiana Territory, first from Spain to France and then from France to the United States, occurred. The event involved ceremonies, a ball, and inspections of the forts that had been built in and near St. Louis. Most of the city's prominent citizens were there to see the Spanish flag taken down and the French flag raised. The next day, the Stars and Stripes flew over St. Louis for the first time.

During the next two and one-half months, the captains finished buying provisions and oversaw the packing of their boats. By the time they began their expedition, they had five boats, a 55-foot-long (17-m-long) keelboat, two smaller flat-bottomed boats known as pirogues, and two large canoes. Finally, on May 21, 1804, the Corps of Discovery started up the Missouri River. The keelboat carried the bulk of their equipment and other goods. It was armed with a swivel gun, which was a cannon mounted on a platform that was just a

The Louisiana Purchase consisted of a three-part agreement between France and the United States. One part was the agreement for France to give the stated territory to the United States. The other two parts described the monetary exchanges between the countries. This case contains the United States' agreement to transfer money in the form of French currency. The agreement is signed by Napoléon Bonaparte.

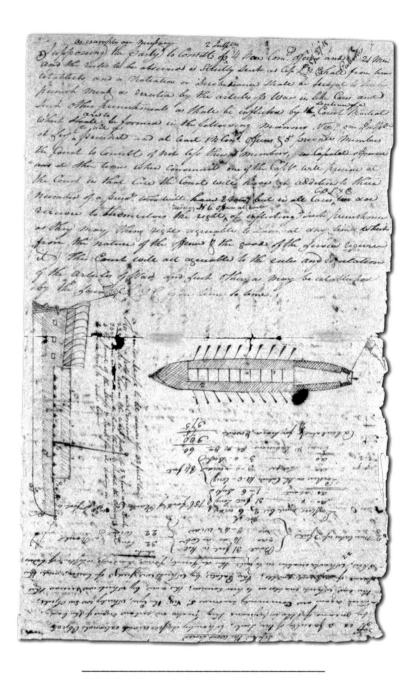

Clark sketched the keelboat in his journal on January 21, 1804. The construction of the keelboat was a frustrating process. The boatbuilder worked slowly and was often too drunk to work at all. Lewis wrote, "Neither threats, persuasion or any other means . . . were sufficient to procure the completion of the work. . . ."

little bigger than the gun. A man standing behind the gun could spin the platform around to aim the gun in any direction. If the wind was right, the keelboat could be sailed up the river, but if there was no wind or the current was too swift, the men had to row. If the river was not deep enough for them to row, they stuck iron poles into the river bottom and pushed the boat upstream. In the worst cases, the men had to pull the boat up the river as they walked along the shore.

The smaller boats were easier to handle, but none of them were completely safe from the dangers of the river. The Missouri River wound through forests, between steep bluffs, and past lush meadows. The explorers had set out in early March, when the muddy water was at its highest point of the season, and huge trees that had been washed away from the banks upriver came roaring downriver toward the travelers. The soldiers in the keelboat had to move from one side of the boat to the other to help it turn aside from such dangers. Those in the smaller boats could simply shift their weight from side to side, in the same way that people steer canoes today.

To make matters worse, the party was plagued by insects, especially mosquitoes, ticks, and gnats. The travelers' diet was limited to hominy, lard, and whatever fresh meat they could get by hunting. They had practically no fruits or vegetables, which caused many of the soldiers to suffer from scurvy, a disease caused by a lack of vitamin C.

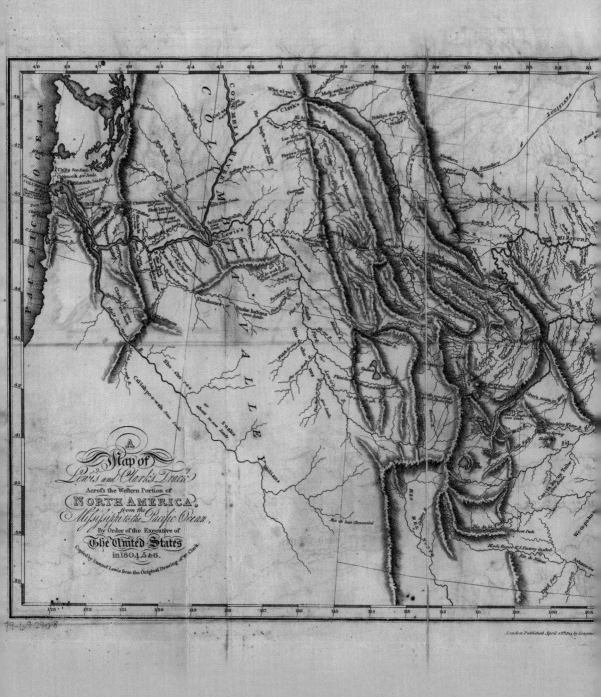

A
Map of
Lewis and Clark's Track
Across the Western Portion of
NORTH AMERICA.
from the
Mississippi to the Pacific Ocean,
By Order of the Executive of
The United States
in 1804, 5 & 6.
Copied by Samuel Lewis from the Original Drawing of W.r Clark.

London Published April 1834 by Longman

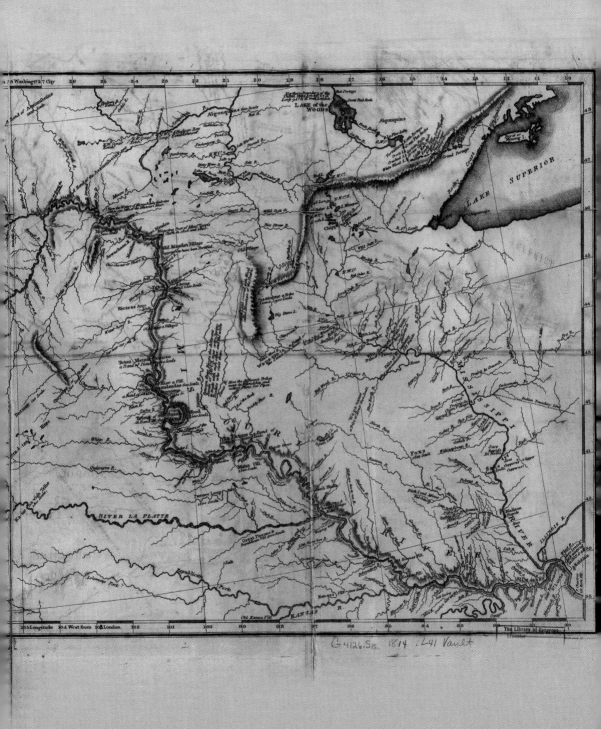

One of the most important goals of the expedition was to establish diplomatic relationships with the Indian nations living in the territory. Jefferson had given Lewis and Clark strict orders to avoid conflict with the Indians. The captains would be dealing with some peoples whom no Americans had ever met before. They were uncertain about what they might encounter as they moved upriver. While they hoped to meet Indians to talk and trade with, they feared being taken by surprise. At night, the Corps camped on islands whenever they could, to lessen the possibility of their being attacked by Indians who saw the Americans as intruders. They also took turns guarding the camp so that they would be aware of any possibility of attack.

They reached the mouth of the Platte River without seeing a single Indian. This was a distance of 600 miles (965.6 km) from their starting point at Fort Wood. The Pawnee and the Sioux who lived in that area were on the plains hunting buffalo. The low mountains of what is now Missouri were behind the Corps, and they were on the beautiful, grassy prairie. It seemed to them that they had found the Garden of Eden that they had expected to see. Though they were disappointed that they had not met any Indians, they were very pleased

Previous spread: This 1814 map is a copy of one drawn by Clark, created from the sketches he made during the expedition. The map shows the Corps' route from the Mississippi River to the Pacific Ocean. Whenever the Corps encountered Indians, Clark talked to them about the lands that lay before the Corps. He used this information to create his maps.

to find the prairies filled with deer, buffalo, and elk, as well as with berries and other fruits. The captains celebrated the Fourth of July by ordering the cannon to be fired and by issuing the soldiers an extra gill of whiskey. One gill equals 4 ounces (11.8 cl) of liquid.

Throughout the trip, both captains continued to write in their journals. Clark, who was a talented mapmaker, regularly drew maps in his journal. All along the way, he recorded the lands through which they passed. Whenever the expedition met with Indians, Clark talked to them about what lay ahead, and he drew maps that included the land features the Indians had described.

Finally, on August 2, well north of the Platte River, the Corps met up with a group of Oto and Missouri Indians accompanied by a French trader who also acted as a translator. The Frenchman spoke to George Drouillard, who was of French and Shawnee Indian descent. Drouillard then repeated his words in English to the explorers. The captains gave the Indians some tobacco, and the Indians gave them watermelons in exchange. The captains invited the Indians to a council the next day. It took place at Council Bluff, which is across the river from present-day Council Bluffs, Iowa. The bluff is a very prominent feature of the landscape there, and many Indian nations had used it as a meeting place.

This meeting with the Oto nation was typical of the way that the Corps of Discovery conducted itself with

John Neagle painted *Caussetongua, or Big Kansas, of the Ottoe Tribe; and Sharitarishe, Chief of the Grand Pawnees* in 1821. The painting shows these two men dressed similarly to how Oto and Pawnee people would have been dressed when the Corps met these groups while travelling through the area now known as Iowa.

the Indians. The captains appeared in their full-dress uniforms, the soldiers marched in step, and they fired off their guns. The point of these activities was to impress the Indians with the wealth and power of the United States. Then Captain Lewis gave a speech. He advised the Indians that they were ruled by a new "Great Chief of the seventeen nations" who had replaced the Spanish and the French officials. He told the Indians that they must not interfere with traders on the river or quarrel with other Indian tribes. He also told them to avoid dealing with men who did not recognize the United States as the ruler of the lands. He said if they did not, the Great Father, President Jefferson, would stop all trade on the river entirely. Lewis promised to open a trading post at the mouth of the Platte River for the Oto and the Missouri if they did as he said.

Then he gave each Indian chief a breechclout, some paint, and either a peace medal with Thomas Jefferson's likeness on it or a comb. The Indians accepted these token gifts graciously, but what they really wanted was gunpowder. Lewis and Clark realized this, but they were hesitant to give the Indians anything they might then

The practice of giving peace medals to Native American chiefs began in the 1790s and continued into the 1880s. The front of the Jefferson peace medals that Lewis and Clark carried showed an image of Jefferson *(left)*. The back showed a handshake and a tomahawk crossed by a peace pipe *(right)*.

use against other Indian nations or white traders or settlers. The Oto and the Missouri told Lewis that they had heard what he said and would take his advice. Then they asked for gunpowder and whiskey, and Lewis consented. After the Indians had received their gifts, he gave a demonstration of his air gun. This weapon was powered by compressed air, so when it was fired it was practically silent. The display amazed the Indians.

Lewis and Clark believed, as did many Europeans and Americans of their time, that Indians were "noble savages." They believed that Native Americans were similar to whites in mind and body, but that they needed to be taught to adapt to the ways of white people, who knew the best possible way to live. Specifically, the captains wanted the Indians to abandon their traditional religions and ways of life to become Christians and to farm for a living, as most white people of that time did. During their previous military service, both Lewis and Clark had encountered Indians who lived in the Ohio River valley, but what the explorers did not understand is that each Indian nation is unique. Sometimes the differences between nations are not great, but more often than not they are significant. Lewis and Clark knew nothing at all about the customs, language, and histories of the peoples they were meeting on their trip, and that lack of knowledge affected how well they dealt with the various Indian nations.

In 1832, George Catlin painted *Floyd's Grave*. Clark wrote of Floyd's death in his journal, "Floyd Died with a great deal of Composure . . . This man at all times gave us proofs of his firmness and Determined resolution to doe Service to his Countery and honor to himself."

The expedition moved up the river. Sometime around the middle of August, Sergeant Charles Floyd became ill, and he got worse with every passing day. Lewis believed that Floyd had what the captain described as "bilious colic," most likely an infected or ruptured appendix, for which there was no treatment. Floyd died on August 20. The captains buried Sergeant Floyd high on a hill overlooking a river that they named Floyd's River. They gave him full military honors, and marked his grave with a red-cedar post. Floyd was the only member of the Corps of Discovery who lost his life on the journey from St. Louis to the Pacific Ocean and back.

Lewis and Clark had been expecting all along that they would meet with members of the Sioux nation, which had the reputation for being the most warlike of any of the Indians west of the Mississippi. On August 27, the Corps met a few Yankton Sioux, and two days later the explorers held a council with a group of them, close to what today is Yankton, South Dakota. That encounter went reasonably well, considering that neither the Indians nor the Corps really understood one another. The next meeting, with the Teton Sioux near what today is Pierre, North Dakota, was a disaster. The Indians had controlled travel on the river for years. They expected to be paid a toll to let the Corps pass through their land. They were disappointed in the presents they received and unimpressed by the speeches Lewis made. The Indians attempted to keep the Corps from traveling upriver, and the men of the Corps resisted. Only the calm, diplomatic intervention of the Sioux chief Black Buffalo prevented bloodshed.

The expedition moved on, passing through Indian villages that were deserted. Several tribes had nearly been wiped out by diseases such as smallpox, measles, and cholera, which they had contracted from whites. In October, in an area that today is near Washburn, North Dakota, the Corps of Discovery came to the villages of

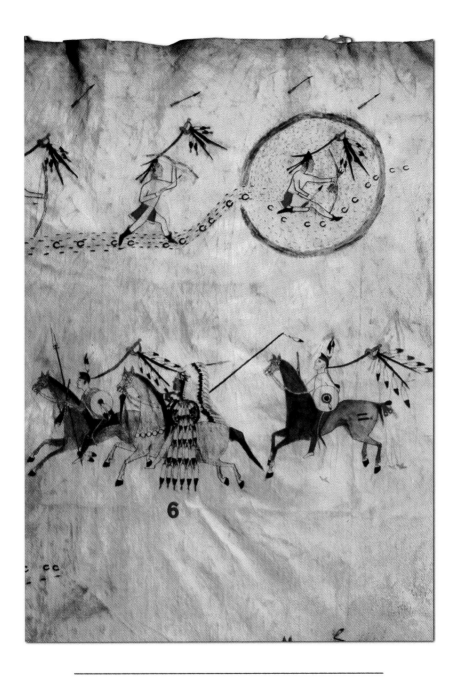

This nineteenth-century Sioux hide painting depicts a battle between Sioux and Blackfeet Indians. The Sioux had a fierce reputation, and it did not help matters that they and the Corps did not speak a common language. The early tense meetings with Native Americans convinced Lewis and Clark that they needed a translator to travel peacefully.

the Mandan and the Arikara, friendly Indians who lived in permanent homes and farmed and hunted for their livelihoods. The captains decided to stay there for the winter. They built a fort across the river from one of the Mandan villages. Throughout the winter, the soldiers traded with the Mandan for corn, beans, and squash. All the explorers were working very hard, in very cold conditions, and they needed to eat a lot. Though they had brought much food with them, they might have run out during that long, cold winter if the Mandan had not been willing to trade with them.

The soldiers named the place Fort Mandan, and there the captains hired a French Canadian trader, Toussaint Charbonneau, as a guide. Charbonneau had once worked as a trapper, but he was then living among the Hidatsa Indian nation. Charbonneau had two Shoshone Indian women with him. One was about fifteen years old. She had been kidnapped by the Hidatsa and had been sold to Charbonneau to pay off a gambling debt. Her name was Sacagawea, and she was six months pregnant. She was brought along because she spoke Shoshone and Hidatsa and could be useful as a translator.

Their encounter with the Sioux had convinced Lewis and Clark that they needed to bring translators with them on the rest of their trip. When they met the Shoshone, for instance, Sacagawea could speak to them in her native, or first, language. Then she could translate what the Shoshone said into Hidatsa to Charbonneau,

The U.S. Mint began producing Sacagawea coins in 2000.

Little is known about Sacagawea. She was a Shoshone, born between 1780 and 1790. Around 1800, Sacagawea was captured by Hidatsa Indians. She and another young Shoshone woman were sold to Charbonneau, who married both women in 1804. Charbonneau and Sacagawea joined the Corps in the winter camp of 1804–1805, during which time she gave birth to her son Jean Baptiste.

Throughout the expedition, Sacagawea was a brave and valuable member of the Corps. She smoothed negotiations with the Indians. Her presence among the men was seen as a "token of peace" by many of the Native American people the Corps visited.

In 1812, a woman identified as Charbonneau's wife died in Fort Manuel, South Dakota. Many people think she was Sacagawea, although some believe that she was Charbonneau's other wife.

who could in turn relay the words to Drouillard in French. Drouillard could then tell the explorers in English what Charbonneau said. This chain of translation would prove awkward and time consuming, but it was better than not having any way to speak with the Indians they met.

In February 1805, Sacagawea gave birth to a son. The boy was named Jean Baptiste Charbonneau, and he would become the youngest member on the trip to the Pacific Ocean.

Once again the captains were waiting for winter to pass. They spent a lot of time writing letters to family and friends and reports for Jefferson. They planned to send the keelboat and some of the men back to St. Louis when spring came. This would be their last chance to send mail east for a long time, so they wanted to take advantage of it. They were looking westward, to the next part of their journey, but the long winter gave them plenty of time to think about what they had experienced so far, and the people they had left behind them.

6. Fort Mandan to the Pacific Ocean

On April 7, 1805, Captains Meriwether Lewis and William Clark sent six soldiers back to St. Louis on the keelboat. The upper reaches of the Missouri River were too narrow and shallow for the keelboat to be of further use. The keelboat began the journey downstream packed with botanical and mineral specimens, the captains' reports and letters to Thomas Jefferson, and two live animals, a magpie and a prairie dog, for the president. In two pirogues and six canoes, the rest of the expedition headed north against the current of the Missouri River.

North of Fort Mandan, the river veered almost directly west, into what is now Montana. The explorers passed through a broad prairie, but by mid-May they could see the first peaks of the Rocky Mountains to the West. Around the seventh of June, about halfway across what has become Montana, the Corps reached the mouth of the Marias River. There they packed some supplies into one of the pirogues and buried the whole boat in a cache so that they would have reserves in a place that they were certain to pass by on the return

Karl Bodmer (1809–1893) painted *The Missouri, Below the Mouth of the Platte* in 1833. This location is near present-day Plattsmouth, Nebraska. Bodmer, like George Catlin, set out to document the people and the landscapes of the rapidly-transforming American West without romanticizing his subject matter.

trip. A few days farther on, they reached Great Falls of the Missouri River.

Lewis was very impressed with the falls, which include five separate cascades. He wrote a vivid description of the rapids in his journal. Clark measured the first, and highest, cascade, at about 80 feet (24.4 m) from the top of the falls to the water below. The men knew that going over the falls in boats would be impossible. They would have to carry most of their provisions and their canoes around the cascades. They cached

Clark sketched this map of the Great Falls and Portage of the Missouri River, in what is today's Montana, on July 4, 1805. During this time, the Corps were building new boats and also celebrating their nation's twenty-ninth birthday.

more supplies above the falls in the second pirogue and then started off.

Lewis and Clark intended to keep going up the Missouri River because its headwaters marked the northern limit of the Louisiana Territory, and they wanted to make sure of exactly where this limit lay on the land so that they could map it. They also knew that Sacagawea's people, the Shoshone, lived close to the headwaters, and they wanted to trade with the Indians for horses.

Below the falls, Lewis set the men to assembling the iron boat that they had brought all the way from Pittsburgh. Lewis had planned to cover it with elk and buffalo hides. Despite their efforts, the boat initially floated but then leaked and sank. The soldiers pulled it out of the water, but it was obvious that the boat would never float. Lewis was forced to abandon a cherished plan, and the soldiers had to spend several days building two dugout canoes from cottonwood trees. They cached the iron boat on shore by Great Falls and started on their way again in mid-July.

As they paddled and poled up the river, the explorers could plainly see snowcapped mountains in the distance, but the plains they were crossing were hot and treeless. They continued to see huge herds of buffalo, and Lewis described the bighorn sheep and the western meadowlark in his journals. He was the first American to do so. The Corps recorded 178 plants and 122 animals that had never been seen by people back east.

Clark drew this bighorn sheep on May 25, 1805. Members of the expedition wrote descriptions or drew pictures of the animals they encountered on their journey. They also captured and killed animals either for food or to send back east as specimens. The head of one of the sheep they killed weighed 27 pounds (12.2 kg)!

The captains were anxious to find the Shoshones. Therefore, starting in the second week in July, they alternated leading a small group of the men on the shore. This group went ahead of the rest of the Corps, which was traveling by water. Lewis went first, but he didn't meet any Indians. On July 19, Clark led the land party, and Lewis stayed with the boats. That day, they reached a ridge of mountains that Lewis named the Gates of the Rocky Mountains. The group on the boats proceeded into the canyon, which led them into

Lewis described the Gates of the Rocky Mountains as the "most remarkable clifts we have yet seen. . . . every object here wears a dark and gloomy aspect. the towering and projecting rocks in many places seem ready to tumble on us." This photograph was taken by Francis D. Jones in 1890.

a beautiful valley. On both sides of the valley, the mountains loomed.

The explorers were unprepared for how high and rugged those mountains were. They had believed that there was one low range of mountains to cross, and that on the other side the Corps would find a long, flat plain, similar to the one they had crossed as they traveled through what is now Kansas, Nebraska, and the Dakotas. They believed that soon they would come on the river that would take them straight to the Pacific Ocean. They could see, however, that the mountains before them were far higher than those they had expected. The mountains were the Rocky Mountains, the highest mountains any American had seen on the continent.

Their hopes of an easy passage were dashed, and they knew that they would have to abandon their canoes. Now they were nearly desperate to acquire horses. They kept moving, traveling several miles (km) each day, but still they found no Indians. Finally, on August 9, Lewis again set out ahead of the rest of the party. He took his guide George Drouillard and two other men. After four days of traveling into the mountains, Lewis's party crossed a mountain pass, a ravine leading to the foot of a mountain, which people or animals can follow to the top of the mountain ridge. Then the party traveled down the other side. Today this pass is known as Lemhi Pass. It is located on what is now the Montana-Idaho border. At the top of the Continental Divide, Lewis and his men saw range after range of enormous, forbidding mountains.

The part of the Rocky Mountains that the Corps of Discovery was about to enter is now called the Bitterroot Mountains. They stretch down the western part of Montana into Idaho, and the wilderness there is still rugged and untamed. Lewis did not record impressions of the terrain in his journal, but he was probably very discouraged at the sight of those mountains.

Fortunately for the explorers, they met the Shoshone on August 13. The Indians led them into the camp of Chief Cameahwait. The Shoshone provided Lewis with horses, and the men of the Corps started back toward Clark's party with Cameahwait and several other Shoshones in tow. When the two groups met on

August 17, the captains and the Indians began talking. Suddenly Sacagawea jumped up, ran to Cameahwait, and threw her arms around him. He was her brother.

Communicating was complicated. Cameahwait spoke to Sacagawea in Shoshone. She relayed their words to Charbonneau in Hidatsa. Charbonneau then told Private Francis Labiche what had been said in French, and the private told the captains in English. Still, the captains and the Indians soon made an agreement. The Shoshone would lead the Corps of Discovery across the Bitterroot Mountains. Cameahwait provided a guide to take the soldiers into the land of the Nez Percé Indians to the west.

The Corps of Discovery spent several days with the Shoshone, resting, hunting, and preserving meat for their trip. On September 1, they moved on. They met briefly with the friendly Salish Indians, crossed another pass in the Bitterroot Mountains, and then descended the Lolo Trail. This is one of the most treacherous passes in the Rockies. Their path was a well-known Indian road, but it was rough going. The terrain was steep and rocky, and the trail that they had to follow was narrow. Sometimes they had to walk single-file, leading their horses, along ledges that ran along the side of the mountain. On one side stood the hillside, and on the other there was nothing at all to stop them from plunging over the edge. Fallen trees lay across the trail, making progress slow and difficult. Their guide, whom they had nicknamed Old Toby, got lost occasionally. The men were not used to the high altitude, where the air was thinner and drier. At high altitudes, it is harder for people to inhale as much oxygen as they need. To make matters worse, the weather turned bitterly cold, and snow started to fall. The explorers ran out of food and were forced to eat several of their horses to survive.

Finally they emerged from the mountains into a river valley. In the third week of September, they met Nez Percé Indians, who welcomed the Americans. The explorers traded with the Indians for dried fish and camas roots. The explorers talked to the Nez Percé chief, Twisted Hair, about what lay before them. With the help of Nez Percé craftsmen, they spent several days building five new dugout canoes, and, on October 9, 1805, they started down the Clearwater River. Twisted Hair accompanied them.

From there on, their progress was swift. They sometimes traveled more than 20 miles (31 km) per day. They passed through the canyon of the Snake River, which led them to the Columbia River. Here the party encountered the first of a long series of roaring rapids and waterfalls. Along the way they traded with the Nez Percé who lived by the riverbanks. As the party reached the lower stretch of the Columbia, Twisted Hair told the travelers that they would soon be entering the lands of the Chinook people. The Nez Percé and the Chinook were at war, and Twisted Hair

Fort Clatsop was reconstructed in 1955 over the original site near Astoria, Oregon. During the rainy winter the Corps spent at Fort Clatsop, the members worked on their journals. Clark also sketched many of the maps that would later be published.

warned Captains Lewis and Clark that his relatives had told him that the Chinook intended to kill the Americans when they arrived. Here Twisted Hair left the explorers. If he continued into the land of the Chinook, he told them, his enemies would kill him. The Americans continued their journey westward.

The culture of the Chinook people was entirely different from any the captains had experienced, and none of their translators could talk to the Indians. Neither this nor Twisted Hair's warning, however, stopped the captains from trading goods for food. In mid-October, the explorers reached The Dalles, a series of rapids and waterfalls in Oregon. Many different Indian tribes had fished there for salmon for generations. The Corps of Discovery continued down the river and through the plains of what today are Washington and Oregon States. They then passed through the Cascade Range of the Sierra Nevada.

On November 7, 1805, William Clark wrote in his journal that the Pacific Ocean was in view. What he saw was not actually the ocean, however, but the estuary of the Columbia River. The Corps reached the ocean the next day. They built a fort, Fort Clatsop, near what is now Astoria, Oregon, and settled in for the winter. They were hoping that a European ship might appear and take back reports of their success, or possibly even take some of the party back, but during the long winter no ship arrived.

Their winter camp was cold and wet, and the Clatsop Indians were not very impressed with the Americans. The Clatsop were the most numerous Indians along that stretch of the Pacific coast. They had long been trading with the English and other Europeans whose ships stopped along the coast from time to time. Compared with the rich supplies the ships carried, none of the goods that the captains had to barter interested the Indians, who were tough bargainers. The relationship between the Americans and the Indians got worse as the winter wore on.

This was probably the most miserable time the Corps of Discovery endured during the entire 2,000-mile (3,218.7-km) trip. They had reached the ocean and could go nowhere until spring came and the snow on the mountains to the east melted. It rained almost constantly. The men of the Corps spent the time waiting impatiently for spring to begin.

7. Back to St. Louis

On March 23, 1806, with practically all their supplies used up, the Corps of Discovery headed east up the Columbia River in canoes. It was early in the season to be traveling, and they were not finding much game. All along the way they had to deal with Indians stealing things from them. At one point, three Indians stole Meriwether Lewis's dog, Seaman. This made Lewis furious, and only the fact that the Indians gave the dog back kept him from becoming violent.

When they got past The Dalles in mid-April, the explorers left the river and headed for the Nez Percé villages to buy horses for the overland journey. On April 27, they met up with a group of Wallawalla, who were related to the Nez Percé, near the junctions of the Columbia and Snake rivers. They stayed there a few days, resting and trading for horses and food.

The weather turned cold and rainy as they started for Twisted Hair's village. Upon their arrival on May 4, they met more of the Nez Percé leaders, including Cut Nose and Broken Arm. Here the Corps of Discovery waited for the snows on the Lolo Trail to melt. In the meantime, they held councils with the Nez Percé leaders and promised them the friendship of the United States. The captains also invited several of the Indians to travel to Washington, D.C., to meet the president.

Lewis and Clark also offered to negotiate peace between the Nez Percé and the Blackfeet, who were traditionally enemies. If Lewis and Clark had succeeded, the Nez Percé could have hunted buffalo east of the Rocky Mountains. This diplomatic effort came to nothing, as did most of the captains' attempts at brokering peace between Native American groups.

The Indians warned the Corps of Discovery that the snow on the Lolo Trail was still too deep for them to pass, but the explorers were impatient to get home, so they started out anyway on June 15. Just a few days later, Lewis and Clark sent two of their soldiers back to the Nez Percé village to ask for a guide. The rest of the party waited anxiously for five days until the soldiers returned with help. When they set off again, they crossed the mountains in about half the time it had taken the year before. They reached the spot that Clark had named Travellers Rest, which is at the junction of Lolo Creek and the Bitterroot River in present-day Montana, on June 30.

After resting for a few days, Clark took part of the Corps south along the Yellowstone River, and Lewis went up the Blackfoot River and then overland to the Great Falls. They were still looking for the elusive

Clark etched his name on a "remarkable rock" on the south bank of the Yellowstone River, near Billings, Montana. He called the rock Pompy's Tower in honor of his nickname for Sacagawea's son, Jean Baptiste, whom he called Little Pomp.

Northwest Passage, and they knew that this was their last chance to find it.

Lewis's group crossed the high plains, hunting buffalo as they went. When they reached the Great Falls, they dug up the supplies they had buried there the year before. At the Great Falls they separated yet again, and Lewis led a few soldiers along the Marias River. Clark took the rest southeast to explore the Yellowstone River area. Lewis ended up in the area just south of present-day Glacier National Park.

On July 27, Lewis and his companions had an unfortunate encounter with a small band of Piegan hunters. The Piegan are one of three groups of the Blackfeet. When the Indians tried to steal the explorers' weapons and horses, Lewis and one of his men killed two of the Indians. The explorers rushed back to the Missouri River, loaded their gear into their boats, and took off down the river as fast as they could go to avoid retaliation from the Piegan.

Meanwhile, Sacagawea led Clark's party over what is now Bozeman Pass, Montana. Crow Indians stole half of the party's horses, but the group found the Yellowstone

This undated photograph of Bozeman Pass, taken by Herman Schnitzmeyer, shows Northern Pacific Railroad tracks, which were laid in the 1870s. The landscape, however, looks much as it would have looked when the Corps first saw it.

River, built some dugout canoes, and went downriver to meet Lewis. Where the two rivers met, Lewis found a note from Clark that said he had gone on ahead. On August 12, just east of what is now the border between Montana and North Dakota, the two groups reunited. Lewis had been shot in the hip in a hunting accident, and, although the injury was not life threatening, he was extremely uncomfortable. He had to ride on his stomach in the canoe to keep from hurting himself more.

With the current carrying the light boats, the trip down the river to the Mandan villages took only two days. There John Colter, one of the soldiers, asked for and received the captains' permission to join two fur trappers who were going back up the Missouri River. Colter eventually became well known as the first American to explore what is today Yellowstone National Park. Toussaint Charbonneau was paid for his services, and he, Sacagawea, and one-year-old Jean Baptiste left the Corps of Discovery to stay on with the Mandan.

The rest of the Corps of Discovery left for St. Louis on August 17. They managed to visit with the Arikara without meeting up with the Teton Sioux, with whom they had had a disasterous encounter before. They did run across a band of friendly Yankton Sioux who, at the captains' request, had sent one of their chiefs to Washington, D.C., the previous year. They also began to meet American traders who were going upstream to trap fur and trade with the Indians. The explorers were nearly out of supplies, so they traded for tobacco, whiskey, and flour. The captains were glad to get these goods, but they were not altogether happy to see more traders coming into the area.

On September 21, 1806, the Corps of Discovery reached the European settlements just north of St. Louis. Upon their return, the captains were hailed as heroes.

8. Journey's End

Meriwether Lewis and William Clark spent two months in St. Louis writing reports for Thomas Jefferson and socializing. They were invited to stay in the home of Pierre Chouteau, one of the most prominent citizens of St. Louis. They attended many parties, where they were closely questioned about the places they had seen and the Indians they had encountered on their journey. Fur trading was an important business in St. Louis, and the explorers were asked about the possibilities for expanding this trade into the western lands Lewis and Clark had crossed.

The captains immediately sent a letter to George Rogers Clark, William's brother in Clarksville, Indiana Territory, telling him of their return and their successes. Because William Clark thought that Lewis was a better writer than he, Lewis drafted the letter, and Clark copied and signed it. The captains knew that George Rogers Clark would share the letter with his local newspaper. The story would be picked up by all of the major newspapers to the east of Kentucky. Word of

By the last Mails.

MARYLAND.   BALTIMORE, OCT. 29, 1806.

A LETTER from *St. Louis (Upper Louisiana),* dated *Sept.* 23, 1806, announces the arrival of Captains LEWIS and CLARK, from their expedition into the interior.—They went to the *Pacific Ocean ;* have brought fome of the natives and curiofities of the countries through which they paffed, and only loft one man. They left the *Pacific Ocean* 23d March, 1806, where they arrived in November, 1805 ;—and where fome American veffels had been juft before.—They ftate the Indians to be as numerous on the *Columbia* river, which empties into the *Pacific,* as the whites in any part of the U. S. They brought a family of the Mandan indians with them. The winter was very mild on the *Pacific.*— They have kept an ample journal of their tour ; which will be publifhed, and muft afford much intelligence.

————

Mr. ERSKINE, the new Britifh Minifter to the United States, is warmly attached to the U. States. He married, about feven years fince, an American lady, daughter of Gen. CADWALLADER, of *Pennfyl-vania.* He has a daughter now in the U. States.

Although the Corps returned to St. Louis on September 23, 1806, this article announcing their return did not appear in the Boston *Columbian Centinel* until October 29. Before the telegraph and the telephone, which were invented later in the nineteenth century, it often took several weeks for news to be published in the newspaper.

their success would reach the East Coast through the chain of newspaper reports long before the captains' mail would.

While the captains were finishing up their reports, one of the men, Private Robert Frazier, came to Lewis and asked his permission to publish the journal that Frazier had kept on the journey. Lewis agreed, but later, when he read a description of the book, he got very upset. He could see that Frazier's book would compete with the publication of his own journal, so he wrote to the publishers and demanded that they leave out certain parts of Frazier's book. The publishers did not reply to Lewis, but they never published Frazier's journal. Since then Frazier's original manuscript and his views on the experience of traveling with the expedition have been lost.

Early in November, the captains left St. Louis on their way to Washington, D.C. They were escorting Mandan Indian chief Big White and his family. Big White had been the chief of one of the villages located near the area where the expedition had spent its first winter. Big White's people had been very helpful to the explorers, and he had agreed to go east with them to visit Thomas Jefferson. When they reached Frankfort, Kentucky, Lewis and the Indian delegation headed for Washington, D.C., and Clark went to Fincastle, Virginia. He was planning to visit friends there, but he also wanted to court Julia Hancock. Hancock, who was Clark's cousin, was the daughter of a prominent

Virginian family. She was sixteen that year. Now that he had met his obligations to the president and the Corps of Discovery, Clark was anxious to marry and start a family of his own.

Because newspapers all across the country had by then published accounts of the trip, Lewis and his party were the guests of honor in practically every settlement through which they passed. Consequently, the group did not reach Lewis's home at Locust Hill until mid-December. Lewis had not seen his family in more than three years. The townspeople held a dinner in his honor in a local tavern. Then Lewis and his group left for Washington, D.C.

Lewis met with Thomas Jefferson at the President's House on New Year's Day. Three and one-half years had passed since Lewis had left, and of course there had been no guarantee that he would return at all. No one recorded what the two men said to each other, but certainly they were delighted to be together again. Jefferson undoubtedly asked Lewis about the lands, peoples, plants, and animals that he had seen, and Lewis, no doubt, gave him a full and thrilling report.

There were many details to take care of in Washington. Lewis had to write reports to the president and to Congress and make recommendations for compensation for all the men of the Corps. For their labor and heroism, the captains were rewarded with money and land grants.

For their services, the other members of the Corps also received cash payments and land. In addition, Lewis was appointed governor of the Louisiana Territory, which would require him to live in St. Louis.

Lewis's plans for his journals suffered a serious setback in March 1807, when he heard that Sergeant Patrick Gass, one of the men of the Corps, was about to publish a sample of his own account of the expedition. Lewis responded by writing a letter to the *National Intelligencer*, complaining that Gass's book was not

C.B.J. Févret de Saint-Mémin made this watercolor portrait of Lewis in 1807. Lewis is shown wearing Indian-style dress. He is adorned with what might have been white weasel tails that Sacagawea gave to Clark as a Christmas present in 1806.

authorized and most likely would be full of falsehoods. This time, however, the publisher went ahead with the book. He even wrote a reply to Lewis's letter, which he also sent to the newspapers, stating that Lewis was not being fair in demanding that his soldiers not publish their journals. Lewis did not reply.

Despite the competition that Gass's book would create, Jefferson still wanted Lewis to publish his and Clark's journals. At the end of March, Lewis went to Philadelphia to work on getting them ready. In 1807, Philadelphia was the center of scientific learning in America and the natural place to work on the manuscript of the book. He found a publisher, John Conrad, who wrote a prospectus, or a description of the book that Lewis planned to publish. Lewis hired J. B. Varnum to circulate the prospectus to the public in hopes of building interest in the book.

In those days, books were sold by subscription, which meant that the author published a description of his book and invited people to buy it before it was produced. Then the money from the book sales was used to pay for the printing and other expenses. Anything left over went to the author and the publisher. Thus it was very important that the prospectus be written so that people would be excited enough about the book to buy it, sight unseen.

Lewis's book was supposed to be published in two volumes, the first describing the journey and the second dealing with the Corps' scientific efforts. He asked Dr. Benjamin Smith Barton, one of the scientists who had prepared him for his journey four years before, to help him with the scientific volume. The doctor happily agreed. Lewis also commissioned artists to illustrate his book. He hired Frederick Pursh to draw pictures of the plants found on the trip. He found an engraver,

James John Barralet, to make drawings of waterfalls, and he found a well-known French portrait painter, C.B.J. Févret de Saint-Mémin, to make portraits of the Indians who had come back east with the Corps.

Along their journey, Lewis and Clark had collected and preserved animal and plant specimens. Many of the Indians that they had met had given them gifts, so they had a sizable collection of pipes, baskets, clothing, and other small items. The captains kept a few for themselves, gave some to Jefferson to display at his home in Virginia, and donated the rest to Charles Willson Peale's museum in Philadelphia.

Peale, who was one of the best artists in the United States at the time, was so delighted with the gift that he started making drawings of the animals for Lewis's book. He also painted a portrait of Lewis that is now in the Independence National Historical Park in Philadelphia. Peale later painted a portrait of Clark that hangs there.

When he was not promoting or working on his book, Lewis spent a lot of his time in Philadelphia going to parties and drinking. He courted several young women, none of whom were interested in marrying him. William Clark, meanwhile, had been successful in persuading Julia Hancock to become his wife. After they married, Clark and his bride settled in Kentucky. In 1807, Clark was made Indian agent for the Louisiana Territory and brigadier general of its militia. This job

Charles Willson Peale drew this woodpecker for Lewis around 1806. Peale's Museum had a wide range of collections. These included gadgets, stuffed animal specimens, and his famous portraits of prominent Americans.

required diplomatic skills, as he was expected to build up the defenses of the territory to protect it from hostile Native American groups while establishing friendly relations with the various Indian groups living in the territory. He moved his household to St. Louis, where he assumed his duties.

Having accomplished very little on the journals, Lewis went back to Washington, D.C., in July and on to Locust Hill to see his family. He finally returned to St. Louis late in the winter of 1808 to take up his post as governor of the Louisiana Territory. He shared a house for a while with Clark and his wife before moving into his own quarters.

Meriwether Lewis had been a very capable and inspiring commander of the Corps of Discovery, but he was terrible as governor of the Louisiana Territory. He was accustomed to giving orders and demanding obedience, a characteristic that did not work well with either his civilian superiors or his employees. In St. Louis, he spent public money liberally and his requests for federal troops to

George Catlin painted this portrait of Clark in 1832. Clark was an Indian agent for the Louisiana Territory from 1807 to 1813. He held the position of Superintendent of Indian Affairs from 1822 through the end of his life in 1838.

deal with unruly Indian tribes struck most people as unnecessary and unreasonable.

He did not do any work at all on the journals. More than once, Jefferson wrote to Lewis asking about his progress on compiling and editing them. As time passed, Jefferson's letters became increasingly sharp. The president was clearly getting irritated with the delays.

Finally, in August 1809, Lewis traveled east to explain his actions to officials in Washington, D.C. He was deeply depressed and fearful about what would happen when he got to the capital. On October 11, at Grinder's Inn, a small, roadside tavern about 70 miles (112.7 km) from Nashville, Tennessee, Meriwether Lewis committed suicide.

Although they were horrified and grief stricken by Lewis's action, neither Thomas Jefferson nor William Clark were particularly surprised by it. It seems they felt that Lewis's melancholy, which both had noticed in the past, had gotten the better of him. In addition, by the time he died, Lewis's drinking had become very serious and probably had contributed to his decision to take his own life.

Both men remained faithful to their friend's memory. Years later, in 1813, Thomas Jefferson wrote about Lewis: "Of courage undaunted, possessing a firmness & perservance of purpose which nothing but impossibilities could divert from it's direction, careful as a father of those committed to his charge, yet steady in the

This monument dedicated to Lewis can be found in Meriwether Lewis
Park on the Natchez Trace Trail in Tennessee. The Trail was a pioneer
trail in the nineteenth century. The monument was erected near the
unmarked grave where Lewis was buried.

maintenance of order & discipline, intimate with the Indian character, customs & principles, habituated to the hunting life, guarded by exact observation of the vegetables & animals of his own country, against losing time in the description of objects already possessed, honest, disinterested, liberal, of sound understanding and a fidelity to truth so scrupulous that whatever he should report would be as certain as if seen by ourselves, with all these qualifications as if selected and implanted by nature in one body, for this express purpose, I could have no hesitation in confiding the enterprise to him." Lewis would not receive such glowing praise again for more than a century.

9. The Legacy of the Corps of Discovery

Meriwether Lewis left a lot of unfinished business that required the attention of his family and friends. After Lewis's death, William Clark stayed in St. Louis as an Indian agent, but he also retrieved the journals and took them to Philadelphia. There he hired a man named Nicholas Biddle to publish them. Biddle wrote a narrative of the journey based on the journals, but the volume of scientific material that Lewis had planned to compile was never published.

By the time Biddle's description of the journey appeared in 1814, however, the Lewis and Clark expedition was old news. An active trade with the tribes that Lewis and Clark had encountered was taking shape, and explorers were creating new maps, filling in the vast areas to either side of the narrow route that the Corps of Discovery had crossed. New names were given to the mountains and rivers that Lewis and Clark had named but had never publicly recorded. Perhaps most important, the great scientific discoveries of the expedition were quickly overshadowed. Other travelers recorded and named the plants and animals that the explorers had first discovered but had never reported. As time passed, the Lewis and Clark expedition lost the heroic stature it had enjoyed upon its return to the United States. Nicholas Biddle's book, published eight years after the explorers returned, was a third-hand account of the journey and included almost none of the critical scientific material that the captains had so painstakingly recorded. As this was the only published record of the journey, few Americans appreciated the importance of what the party had accomplished.

Not until 1904, one hundred years after Lewis and Clark began their journey, was a complete edition of their original journals published. By failing to ensure that his record of the great expedition was published, Meriwether Lewis denied himself recognition as one of the world's great natural scientists. For a century, the journey of the Corps of Discovery was seen as a minor incident in the great American expansion toward the Pacific coast.

Though the captains ultimately failed to accomplish some of their primary goals, the journey itself made Americans aware of the challenges that the young nation would face as it conquered the territory and the peoples who lived in the West. One of President Jefferson's most

Opposite: This map shows the population distribution in the 1890 U.S. census. In the eighty-five years following the expedition, settlers expanded from the lands acquired in the Louisiana Purchase to the Pacific coast. Unfortunately, this expansion displaced Native Americans, many of whom were forcibly relocated to Oklahoma, shown in white.

PLATE 6.

20. DISTRIBUTION OF THE POPULATION OF THE UNITED STATES: 1890.

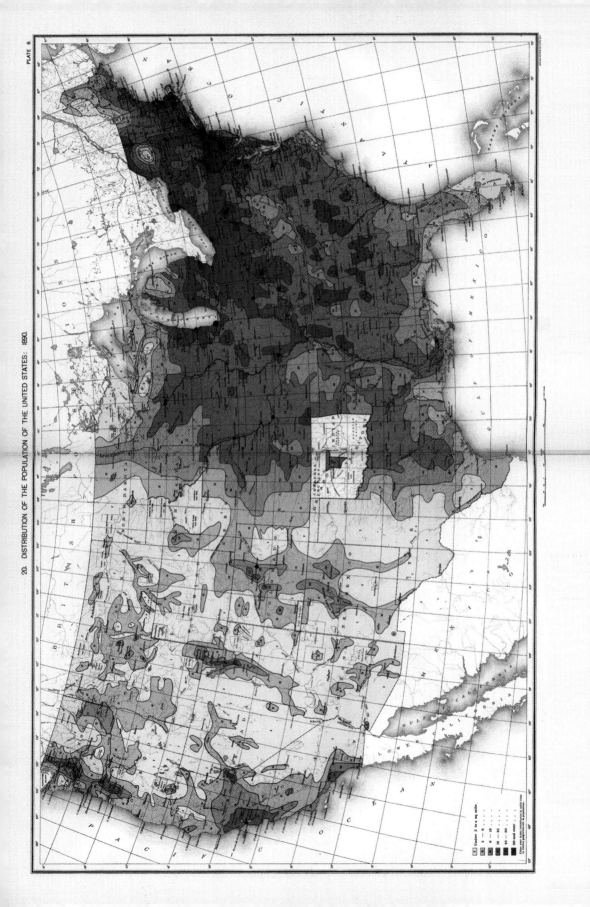

important goals for the Corps of Discovery had been to find the fabled Northwest Passage across the continent. Lewis and Clark did not find this water route, nor did explorers who searched for it after the expedition returned home. The need for such a transcontinental trade route became greater as America expanded into the West. Because a water route did not exist, people on the East Coast were beginning to talk about building a railroad across the continent as early as the 1830s.

After the United States gained control of California and other western lands in a war with Mexico in 1848, Americans began to move into these new western territories. The discovery of gold in California in 1848 also brought a flood of new settlers into the area. Spurred by the prospect of vast

In 1904, St. Louis hosted the World's Fair, officially called the Louisiana Purchase International Exposition. This fair celebrated the one-hundredth anniversary of the Louisiana Purchase. This lithograph by Alphonse Maria Mucha advertised the fair. That same year, the complete journals of Lewis and Clark were published.

western wealth, businessmen from California and the East banded together to build a railroad across the continent. By 1869, only sixty-six years after Lewis and Clark had searched for the Northwest Passage, the railroad was completed. The terminus, however, was Sacramento, California, not the Pacific Northwest. The gold rush had made California much more important to easterners.

The Corps of Discovery's other primary job had been to gather information about the native peoples who lived in the West and convince them of the power of the United States. Jefferson wanted Indians to recognize that America would play a powerful role in the future of the West and that it would be better to have Americans as friends than as enemies. Lewis and Clark were not particularly successful at achieving this aim.

During their travels, Lewis and Clark met a great many Indian tribes that they had not known about before, but it can not be said that they "discovered" those tribes. Many of these Indians had been living on the land for hundreds of years. Because of the ideas they had about Indians, Lewis and Clark were dismal failures at persuading most of the tribes they met to become allies of the United States.

In fact, to most of the Indians that Lewis and Clark met, the explorers' visit was not very important. It made a brief impression on them, and then they went on with their lives. To the tribes of native peoples they encountered, members of the Corps of Discovery were not explorers, but were just an unusual group of travelers. Some Indians simply saw them as trespassers.

All the Indian tribes that Lewis and Clark encountered had different priorities from those of the Americans. A clear indication of this is Lone Dog's winter count. A winter count is a written record in pictures of important events that happened to the artist's tribe, and sometimes to other tribes as well, from one year to the next. Typically, one image appears for each year. Lone Dog was a Sioux Indian. He made his winter count on the back of a tanned animal hide. The document was started in 1800, when Lone Dog noted that the Crow had killed several Sioux. The year that Lewis and Clark passed through Sioux territory, the winter count makes no mention of them. Instead the Indians noted that they had captured some ponies in that year. The last year on the winter count is 1871.

The Lewis and Clark expedition might not have seemed important to the Indians at the time, but in the end it had grave consequences for them. The explorers were just the first of a flood of white Americans coming across the Mississippi River into Native American lands. Lewis and Clark might not have found a Northwest Passage, but they did prove that a trip across the continent, though dangerous, was possible. By doing so, they fired the imaginations of a generation of frontiersmen, fur trappers, traders who wanted the

Indians as customers, and adventurers who sought fortune, fame, or simply excitement in the regions previously known only to the Indians.

Two hundred years after Lewis and Clark set off on their journey, Americans understand the legacy of the Corps of Discovery more completely. We see their mission as a great adventure and an opportunity to learn about lands and peoples foreign to Americans in 1803. Today St. Louis, the westernmost American city in the explorers' day, calls itself the Gateway to the West. The city's Gateway Arch, a great stainless steel sculpture standing on the west bank of the Mississippi River,

Lone Dog kept his winter count from 1800 to 1871. A winter count records history. The winter count is made of cowhide and it reads from the center and spirals outward counterclockwise. Each picture represents an event. For example, a man with a hat stands for a white man and a horseshoe represents a horse.

The Jefferson National Expansion Memorial Arch was designed by
the famous architect Eero Saarinen and was completed in 1965. It
stands 630 feet (192 m) tall and has an elevator that goes to the top of
the arch. A museum is located below the arch and houses artifacts from
the expedition and an overview of the Lewis and Clark expedition.

commemorates Jefferson's purchase of the Louisiana Territory and the journey of the Corps of Discovery. With the benefit of history, we can appreciate the promise that the Louisiana Territory held for the growing United States and understand the feelings of the Indian peoples that the explorers encountered. By learning more about the Lewis and Clark expedition, we can share the adventurous spirit that sent the explorers across the continent, and we can better understand how this important journey helped to create the nation we now know.

Timeline

1770   William Clark is born in Caroline County, Virginia.

1774   Meriwether Lewis is born in Albemarle County, Virginia.

1795   Ensign Lewis is transferred into the Chosen Rifle Company, under Clark's command.

1796   Clark leaves the army and returns to his family home, which today is in Kentucky.

1801   Thomas Jefferson offers Lewis the position of personal secretary.

        Jefferson learns that Spain has given the Louisiana Territory back to France.

1802   Jefferson chooses Lewis to lead the Corps of Discovery to the Pacific Ocean.

1803   Lewis leaves Washington, D.C., for Harpers Ferry, Virginia, to buy arms for the journey.

        In Washington, D.C., Lewis learns that Napoléon Bonaparte sold the Louisiana Territory to the United States for $15 million.

        Lewis meets Clark at Clarksville, Indiana Territory, across the Ohio River from Louisville, Kentucky.

1804   The Corps of Discovery starts to travel up the Missouri River.

        The Corps meets the Teton Sioux, an encounter which nearly ends in violence.

        The Corps of Discovery reaches the Arikara and Mandan villages near what is now Washburn, North Dakota. Lewis and

Clark decide to camp there over the winter.

1805 The expedition continues up the Missouri.

Lewis meets Shoshone Indians led by Cameahwait, brother of Sacagawea.

The Corps of Discovery starts down the Clearwater River, on their way to the Pacific Ocean.

The explorers sight the estuary of the Columbia River.

1806 The Corps starts across the Lolo Trail.

Guided by Nez Percé Indians, the Corps begins to cross the Lolo Trail for the second time.

The Corps of Discovery reaches the European settlements just north of St. Louis.

1807 Lewis is appointed governor of the Louisiana Territory.

Clark is appointed Indian agent for the Louisiana Territory.

1809 Lewis commits suicide at Grinder's Inn, outside Nashville, Tennessee.

1814 Nicholas Biddle's edition of the Lewis and Clark journals is published.

1822 Clark is made Superintendent of Indian Affairs.

1838 Clark dies.

Glossary

American Revolution (uh-MER-uh-ken reh-vuh-LOO-shun) Battles that soldiers from the colonies fought against Britain for freedom, from 1775 to 1783.

anthropology (an-thruh-PAH-luh-jee) The study of human beings in relation to distribution, origin, classification, and relationship of races, physical character, culture, and environmental and social relations.

architecture (AR-kih-tek-cher) The art of creating and making buildings.

armory (ARM-ree) A place where arms and ammunition are stored.

Articles of Confederation (AR-tih-kulz UV kun-feh-deh-RAY-shun) The laws that governed the United States before the Constitution was created.

botany (BAH-tun-ee) The study of plants.

breechclout (BREECH-clowt) A loincloth.

cache (KASH) A hiding place, usually for food.

celestial navigation (suh-LES-tee-ul na-vih-GAY-shun) The ability to travel by observation of heavenly bodies such as the Sun, the Moon, the stars, and the planets.

cholera (KAH-luh-rah) A very contagious and often fatal intestinal disease.

chronometer (kruh-NAH-meh-ter) A timepiece designed to keep time with great accuracy.

Continental Divide (kon-tin-EN-tul dih-VYD) The watershed in the Rocky Mountains where water falling on the west side drains into the Pacific Ocean, and on the east side drains into the Atlantic

Ocean. In general, the divide runs from north to south through the Rockies, from British Columbia in Canada, southward into Mexico and Central America.

court-martial (KORT-mar-shul) Having to do with a trial held under military, not civilian, authority.

delirium (dih-LIR-ee-um) A mental disturbance characterized by confusion, disordered speech, and hallucinations.

endured (en-DURD) To have undergone hardship without giving up.

Enlightenment (en-LY-ten-ment) A philosophical movement that began in the eighteenth century and was marked by a focus on rationalism and a rejection of traditional social, religious, and political ideas.

ensign (EN-sun) An officer in the army who ranks below a lieutenant.

estuary (ES-choo-wer-ee) An area of water where the tide meets a river.

ethnology (eth-NAH-luh-jee) A scientific study of the origin of human beings and human culture.

expertise (ek-spur-TEEZ) Highly skilled, well-informed opinion or comment.

headwaters (HED-wah-turz) The source of a stream or a river.

hominy (HAH-mih-nee) A type of cornmeal in which the corn has been soaked in lye and then washed to remove the hulls.

integrated (IN-tuh-grayt-ed) To have brought different groups together to form one group.

land grants (LAND GRANTS) Lands given to individuals from a government.

malaria (muh-LAR-ee-uh) A human disease caused by parasites in the red blood cells, which are transmitted by the bite of mosquitoes. It is characterized by periodic attacks of chills and fever.

melancholy (MEH-len-kah-lee) Depressed or sad in spirit.

militia (muh-LIH-shuh) A group of volunteer or citizen soldiers who are organized to assemble in emergencies.

mineralogy (mih-neh-RAH-luh-jee) The science dealing with minerals, their properties, their classification, and distinguishing between them.

Northwest Passage (NORTH-west PA-sij) A water passage once thought to run through North America to China or India.

plantations (plan-TAY-shunz) Very large farms where crops were grown.

prospectus (pruh-SPEK-tes) A printed statement that describes an enterprise, such as a business or a publication, and that is distributed to potential buyers, investors, or participants.

scurvy (SKUR-vee) A disease resulting from a deficiency of vitamin C, characterized by weakness and bleeding from mucous membranes.

sharpshooters (SHARP-shoo-terz) Good marksmen.

smallpox (SMOL-poks) A serious and often fatal sickness that causes a rash and leaves marks on the skin.

specimens (SPEH-sih-minz) Samples.

subscription (sub-SKRIP-shen) An agreement to receive and to pay for something.

swivel gun (SWIH-vul GUN) A cannon mounted on a platform that can spin around, permitting the gun to be aimed in different directions.

temperaments (TEM-pur-ments) Personality characteristics or modes of emotional response.

terminus (TER-mih-nes) Either end of a transportation line or travel route; also, the station, town, or city at such a place.

trespassers (TRES-pas-urz) People who enter another person's property or territory without permission.

undaunted (un-DON-ted) Not easily discouraged; courageous in the face of adversity.

wilderness (WIL-dur-nis) An area that has no lasting settlements.

woodsman (WUDZ-men) A person who frequents or works in the woods, especially one skilled in woodcraft.

zoology (zoh-AH-luh-jee) The study of animals and animal life.

Additional Resources

To learn more about Lewis and Clark and the Corps of Discovery, check out these books and Web sites:

Books

Duncan, Dayton. *Lewis & Clark: The Journey of the Corps of Discovery*. New York, Knopf, 1997.

Gragg, Rod. *Lewis and Clark on the Trail of Discovery: The Journey That Shaped America*. Nashville, TN: Rutledge Hill Press, 2003.

Hunsaker, Joyce Badgley. *Sacagawea Speaks: Beyond the Shining Mountains with Lewis and Clark*. Guilford, CT: Falcon, 2001.

Patent, Dorothy Penshaw. *Animals on the Trail with Lewis and Clark*. New York: Clarion Books, 2002.

Patent, Dorothy Penshaw. *Plants on the Trail with Lewis and Clark*. New York: Clarion Books, 2002.

Web Sites

Due to the changing nature of Internet links, PowerPlus books has developed an online list of Web sites related to the subject of this book. This site is updated regularly. Please use this link to access the list: www.powerkidslinks.com/lalt/lewisclark/

Bibliography

Ambrose, Stephen E. *Undaunted Courage: Meriwether Lewis, Thomas Jefferson, and the Opening of the American West*. New York: Simon & Schuster, 1996.

McCullough, David. *John Adams*. New York: Simon & Schuster, 2001.

Montgomery, M. R. *Jefferson and the Gun-Men. How the West was Almost Lost*. New York: Three Rivers Press, 2000.

Ringle, Ken. "A Young Nation's Growth Spurt." *Washington Post*, Friday, May 2, 2003, C1, C4.

Ronda, James P. *Lewis & Clark Among the Indians*. Lincoln, NE: University of Nebraska Press, 1984.

_____. "The Objects of Our Journey," in, *Lewis and Clark: Across the Divide*, pp. 15–49. Washington, D.C.: Smithsonian Institution Press, 2003.

Steffen, Jerome O. *William Clark: Jeffersonian Man on the Frontier*. Norman: University of Oklahoma Press, 1977.

Index

About the Authors

Michael D. Fox is a specialist in the history of the American West who grew up in Arizona, California, and Wyoming. He studied English and American studies at Humboldt State University in California and at the University of Wyoming. He has worked in the exhibitions and curatorial departments of several museums.

A native of Arkansas, Suzanne G. Fox is a writer, an editor, and a publications project manager. She studied English at Oklahoma Christian College and rhetoric and writing at the University of Tulsa. Among the books she has worked on are *Lewis and Clark: Across the Divide*, *Saddlemaker to the Stars: The Leather and Silver Art of Edward H. Bohlin*, and *How the West Was Worn*.

Michael and Suzanne live in Accokeek, Maryland, near Washington, D.C.

Primary Sources

Cover (background). *Captains Lewis and Clark Holding a Council with the Indians.* Etching, 1810, Patrick Gass, Library of Congress Prints and Photographs Division. **Cover, page 4.** *Meriwether Lewis*, oil-on-canvas painting, around 1807, Charles Willson Peale, Courtesy of Independence National Historical Park, National Park Service. **Cover, page 6.** *William Clark*, oil-on-canvas painting, around 1810, Charles Willson Peale, Courtesy of Independence National Historical Park, National Park Service. **Page 9.** *George Rogers Clark*. Oil-on-canvas painting, around 1830, James Barton Longacre after John Wesley Jarvis, © National Portrait Gallery, Smithsonian Institution / Art Resource, New York. **Page 13.** *Slaves Preparing Tobacco*. Engraving from "Le Costume Ancien et Moderne," Volume II, plate 50, around 1790, by Jules Ferrario, Topkapi Palace Museum, Istanbul, Turkey / Bridgeman Art Library. **Page 14.** *Charge of the Dragoons at Fallen Timbers*. Painting, around 1895, R. T. Zogbaum, The Ohio Historical Society. **Pages 20–21.** *Famous Whiskey Insurrection in Pennsylvania*. Engraving, 1794, anonymous, © The New York Public Library / Art Resource, New York. **Page 24.** Map of North America from the Mississippi River to the Pacific, pen-and-ink with watercolor, 1790s, Library of Congress Geography and Map Division. **Page 27.** *Portrait of Thomas Jefferson*. Oil-on-canvas painting, 1805, Rembrandt Peale, New-York Historical Society, New York, USA/Bridgeman Art Library. **Page 29.** *North Front of the President's House*. Ink-and-wash-on-paper, around 1800, Samuel Blodget Jr., The White House Collection, courtesy the White House Historical Association. **Page 33.** *Napoleon I at Malmaison in 1804*. oil-on-canvas painting, around 1804, François Gérard, © Giraudon / Art Resource, New York. **Page 37.** Compass with Case. National Museum of American History, Smithsonian Institution. **Page 38.** Chronometer. Missouri Historical Society, photograph by Cary Horton. **Page 40.** *The PRAIRIE DOG Sickened at the Sting of the HORNET or a Diplomatic Puppet exhibiting his Deceptions*. Etching with watercolor, 1806, James Akin, Library of Congress Prints and Photographs Division. **Page 43.** Clark's Elkskin-bound journal. Missouri Historical Society. **Page 45.** Louisiana Purchase Treaty Case. 1803, NARA Old Military and Civil Records. **Page 46.** Clark's Field Notes: the Keelboat. 1804, Yale Collection of Western Americana, Beinecke Rare Book and Manuscript Library.

Pages 48–49. A Map of Lewis and Clark's Track Across the Western Portion of North America, from the Mississippi to the Pacific Ocean. 1814, Samuel Lewis from the William Clark original, Library of Congress Geography and Map Division. **Page 52.** *Caussetongua, or Big Kansas, of the Ottoe Tribe; and Sharitarishe, Chief of the Grand Pawnees.* Oil-on-canvas painting, 1821, John Neagle, Courtesy of Historical Society of Pennsylvania Collection, Atwater Kent Museum of Philadelphia/Bridgeman Art Library. **Page 55.** *Floyd's Grave, Where Lewis and Clark Buried Sergeant Floyd in 1804.* Painting, 1832, George Catlin, © Smithsonian American Art Museum, Washington, DC / Art Resource, New York. **Page 57.** Hide Painting Depicting a Battle Between the Sioux and the Blackfoot. Undated, unknown Sioux artist, © Werner Forman / Art Resource, New York. **Page 62.** *The Missouri Below the Mouth of the Platte.* Watercolor-on-paper, 1833, Karl Bodmer, Joslyn Art Museum, Omaha, Nebraska. **Page 63.** Clark's Map of Great Falls and Portage of the Missouri River. 1805, American Philosophical Society. **Page 65.** Bighorn Sheep. Ink on paper, 1805, William Clark, Missouri Historical Society. **Page 66.** Gates of the Rocky Mountains. Photograph, 1890, Francis D. Jones, Montana Historical Society Photograph Archives. **Page 70.** Fort Clatsop National Memorial. Reconstructed fort where the Corps spent the 1805–1806 winter, near Astoria, Oregon. Connie Ricca / CORBIS. **Page 75.** William Clark's signature. Inscribed on Pompy's Tower, near Billings, Montana. July 25, 1806, Montana Historical Society Photograph Archives. **Page 80.** A Letter from St. Louis (Upper Louisiana). Newspaper clipping from the Columbian Centinel in Boston, Massachusetts, October 29, 1806, American Antiquarian Society. **Page 83.** *Merriwether Lewis.* Watercolor-on-paper painting, 1807, C.B.J. Févret de Saint-Mémin, collection of the New-York Historical Society. **Page 86.** Woodpecker, drawn for Capt M. Lewis, Charles Willson Peale. Pencil-on-paper, 1806, Charles Willson Peale, American Philosophical Society. **Page 87.** *William Clark.* Oil-on-canvas painting, 1832, George Catlin, © National Portrait Gallery, Smithsonian Institution / Art Resource, New York. **Page 89.** Meriwether Lewis Monument. Meriwether Lewis Park, Tennessee, Tennessee State Library and Archives. **Page 93.** *Distribution of the Population of the United States: 1890.* Henry Gannett, 1890, Library of Congress Geography and Map Division. **Page 94.** *Exposition Universelle & Internationale de St. Louis.* Lithograph poster, 1903, Alphonse Marie Mucha, Library of Congress Prints and Photographs Division. **Page 97.** *Lone Dog's Winter Count.* 1871, photo courtesy of the South Dakota State Historical Society.

Credits

Photo Credits

Cover left, cover right, pp. 4, 6 courtesy of Independence National Historical Park, National Park Service; cover background, pp. 40, 98 Library of Congress Prints and Photographs Division; p. 9 © National Portrait Gallery, Smithsonian Institution/Art Resource, NY; p. 13 Topkapi Palace Museum, Istanbul, Turkey/Bridgeman Art Library; p. 14 the Ohio Historical Society; p. 15 Military Image Bank; p. 16 from the Portrait Collection of the Jenkins Law Library; pp. 20–21 © The New York Public Library / Art Resource, NY; pp. 24, 48–49, 93 Library of Congress Geography and Map Division; p. 27 New-York Historical Society, New York, USA/Bridgeman Art Library; p. 29 The White House Collection, courtesy the White House Historical Association; p. 33 © Giraudon/Art Resource, NY; p. 36 National Park Service, Harpers Ferry Center Commissioned Art Collection, artist Keith Rocco/Tradition Studios; p. 37 National Museum of American History, Smithsonian Institution; pp. 38, 43, 65 Missouri Historical Society; p. 45 NARA Old Military and Civil Records; p. 46 Yale Collection of Western Americana, Beinecke Rare Book and Manuscript Library; p. 52 courtesy of Historical Society of Pennsylvania Collection, Atwater Kent Museum of Philadelphia/Bridgeman Art Library; p. 53 Oregon Historical Society; p. 55 © Smithsonian American Art Museum, Washington, DC/Art Resource, NY; p. 57 © Werner Forman/Art Resource, NY; p. 62 Joslyn Art Museum, Omaha, NE; pp. 63, 86 American Philosophical Society; pp. 66, 75, 76 Montana Historical Society Photograph Archives; p. 70 © Connie Ricca/CORBIS; p. 80 American Antiquarian Society; p. 83 Collection of the New-York Historical Society; p. 87 © National Portrait Gallery, Smithsonian Institution / Art Resource, NY; p. 89 Tennessee State Library and Archives; p. 94 Library of Congress Prints and Photographs Division; p. 97 photo courtesy of the Museum of the South Dakota State Historical Society.

Project Editors

Gillian Houghton, Jennifer Way

Series Design

Laura Murawski

Layout Design

Corinne L. Jacob, Ginny Chu

Photo Researcher

Jeffrey Wendt

DATE DUE